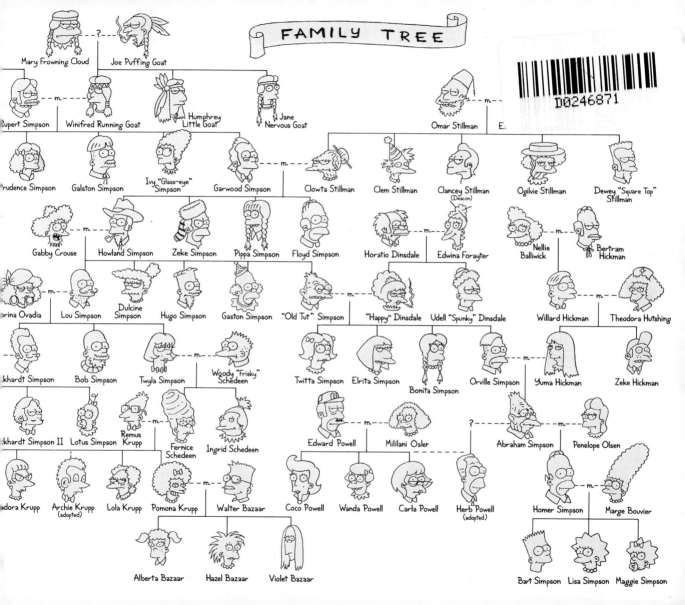

# FAMILY TREE

Mary Frowning Cloud — ? — Joe Puffing Goat

Rupert Simpson — m. — Winifred Running Goat — Humphrey Little Goat — Jane Nervous Goat

Omar Stillman — m. — E.

D0246871

Prudence Simpson — Galston Simpson — Ivy "Glass-eye" Simpson — Garwood Simpson — m. — Clowta Stillman — Clem Stillman — Clancey Stillman (Deacon) — Ogilvie Stillman — Dewey "Square Top" Stillman

Gabby Crouse — m. — Howland Simpson — Zeke Simpson — Pippa Simpson — Floyd Simpson — Horatio Dinsdale — m. — Edwina Forayter — Nellie Balliwick — m. — Bertram Hickman

orina Ovadia — m. — Lou Simpson — Dulcine Simpson — Hugo Simpson — Gaston Simpson — "Old Tut" Simpson — m. — "Happy" Dinsdale — Udell "Spunky" Dinsdale — Willard Hickman — m. — Theodora Hutshing

khardt Simpson — Bob Simpson — Twyla Simpson — m. — Woody "Frisky" Schedeen — Twitta Simpson — Elrita Simpson — Bonita Simpson — Orville Simpson — m. — Yuma Hickman — Zeke Hickman

khardt Simpson II — Lotus Simpson — Remus Krupp — Fernice Schedeen — Ingrid Schedeen — Edward Powell — m. — Mililani Osler — ? — Abraham Simpson — m. — Penelope Olsen

dora Krupp — Archie Krupp (adopted) — Lola Krupp — Pomona Krupp — m. — Walter Bazaar — Coco Powell — Wanda Powell — Carla Powell — Herb Powell (adopted) — Homer Simpson — m. — Marge Bouvier

Alberta Bazaar — Hazel Bazaar — Violet Bazaar

Bart Simpson — Lisa Simpson — Maggie Simpson

MATT GROENING'S

# the SIMPSONS™

## Uncensored Family Album

THE SIMPSONS™ UNCENSORED FAMILY ALBUM

HarperCollins*Entertainment*,
An imprint of HarperCollins*Publishers*
77–85 Fulham Palace Road, Hammersmith, London W6 8JB
www.harpercollins.co.uk

First published in the USA by HarperCollins Publishers, Inc. 1991
This facsimile gift edition published in the UK 2005
1 3 5 7 9 8 6 4 2

ISBN 0 00 721228 3

Printed in Belgium by Proost NV, Turnhout

Concepts, Design & Art Direction: Mili Smythe
Design: Peter Alexander
Design Associate: Barbara McAdams
Family Album Chroniclers: Mary Trainor, Ted Brook
Chronicler Contributor: Jamie Angell
Creative Team: John Adam, Dale Hendrickson, Ray Johnson, Bill Morrison,
Willardson & Associates
Production Assistance: Kim Llewellyn, Dan Chavira
Typesetting: Skil-Set Graphics
Legal Advisor: Susan Grode
Editor: Wendy Wolf

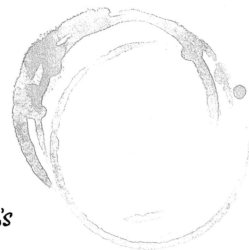

MATT GROENING'S

# tHe SimPSonS™

## Uncensored Family Album

HarperCollins*Entertainment*
*An Imprint of* HarperCollins*Publishers*

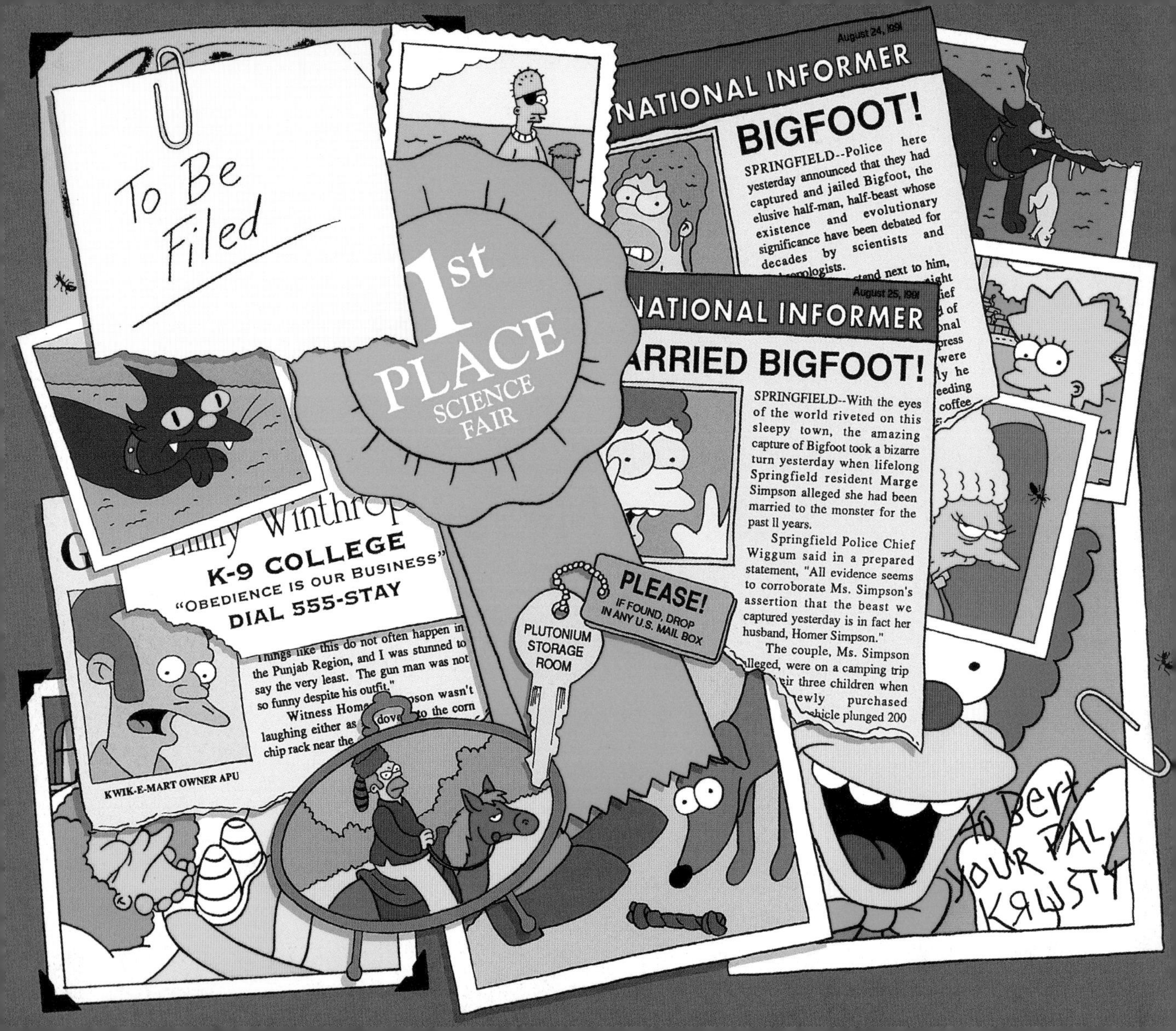
To Be Filed
August 24, 1991
NATIONAL INFORMER
BIGFOOT!
SPRINGFIELD--Police here yesterday announced that they had captured and jailed Bigfoot, the elusive half-man, half-beast whose existence and evolutionary significance have been debated for decades by scientists and
1st PLACE SCIENCE FAIR
August 25, 1991
NATIONAL INFORMER
ARRIED BIGFOOT!
SPRINGFIELD--With the eyes of the world riveted on this sleepy town, the amazing capture of Bigfoot took a bizarre turn yesterday when lifelong Springfield resident Marge Simpson alleged she had been married to the monster for the past 11 years.
Springfield Police Chief Wiggum said in a prepared statement, "All evidence seems to corroborate Ms. Simpson's assertion that the beast we captured yesterday is in fact her husband, Homer Simpson."
The couple, Ms. Simpson
Winthrop
K-9 COLLEGE
"OBEDIENCE IS OUR BUSINESS"
DIAL 555-STAY
the Punjab Region, and I was stunned to say the very least. The gun man was not so funny despite his outfit."
KWIK-E-MART OWNER APU
PLUTONIUM STORAGE ROOM
PLEASE!
IF FOUND, DROP IN ANY U.S. MAIL BOX
To Bert-
YOUR PAL,
KRUSTY

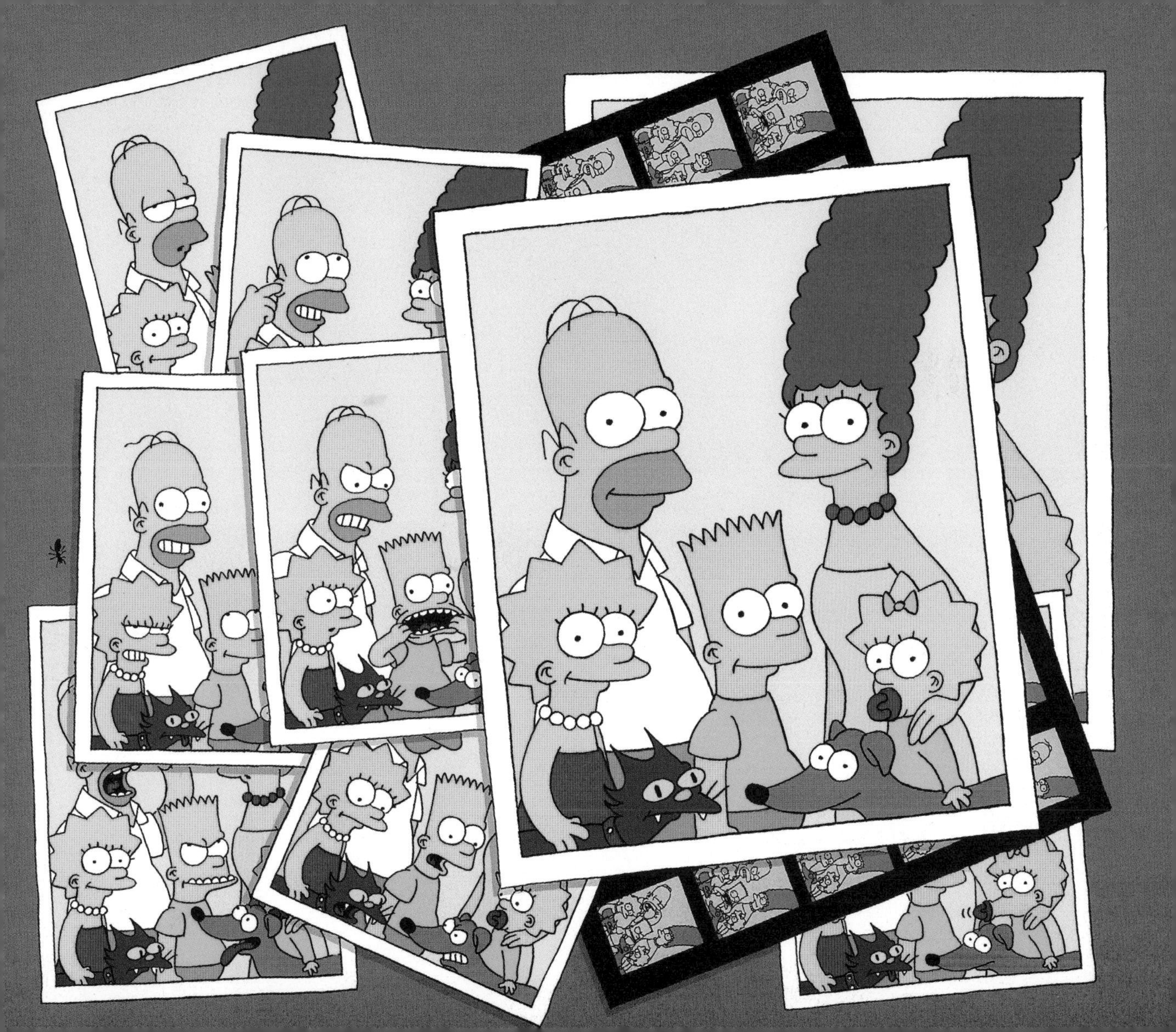

# Where it all began... (at least, as far back as I can trace.)

Great Grandma Bouvier, in her flapper days

Great Grampa Bouvier, right before he shipped out with the Merchant Marines. My grandmother once told me the song "Brandy" was based on his life.

Jo Pepe—
For what it's worth—
Bambi

**Dr. Bouvier's FLESHWORM & BLACKHEAD ERADICATOR $1.00**

↑ One of my Great-great Uncle Charlemagne's "Get-Rich-Quick" schemes

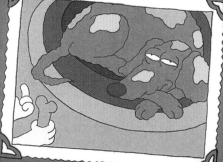

Bouvier Family Picnic, 1903

Great Grandma Bouvier's dog, Fetchy.

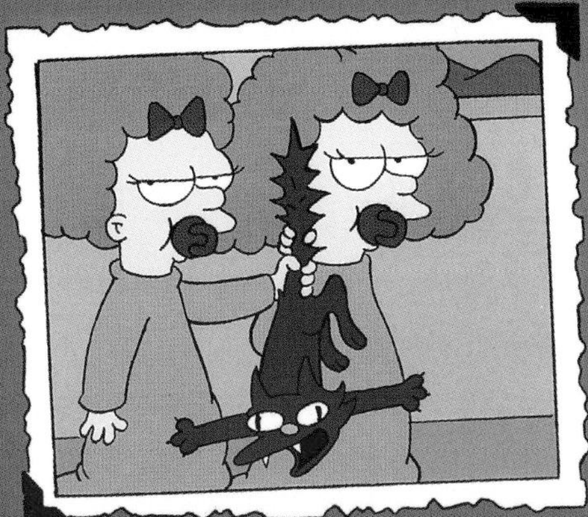

Patty and Selma in their infancy, with our cat, Squirmy.

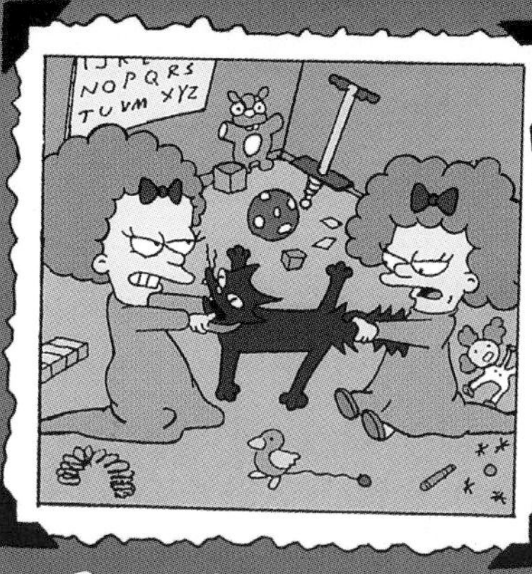

Patty, Selma (age 3½) and Squirmy.

Patty, Selma and me

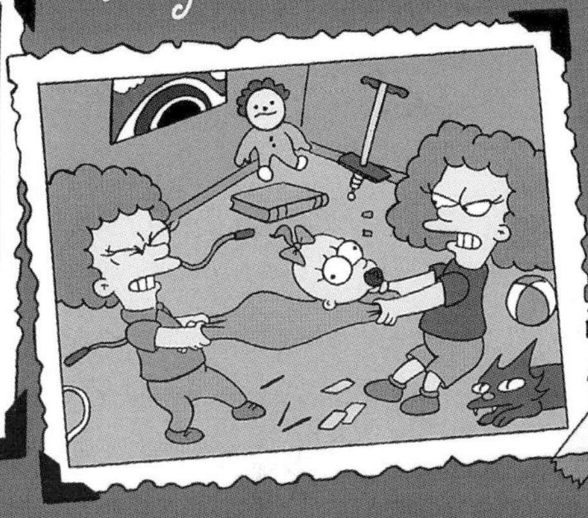

My first book! In the end, the Li'l Gnome grows to be 9 ft. tall. It taught me a valuable lesson about patience, hope and growth!

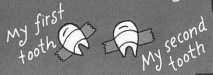

My first tooth

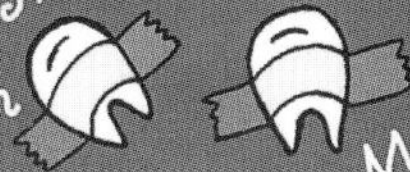

My second tooth

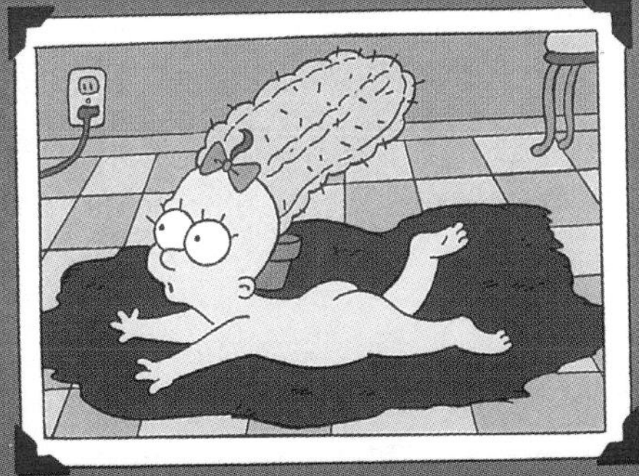

Little Marjorie Bouvier

OOH-WEE!

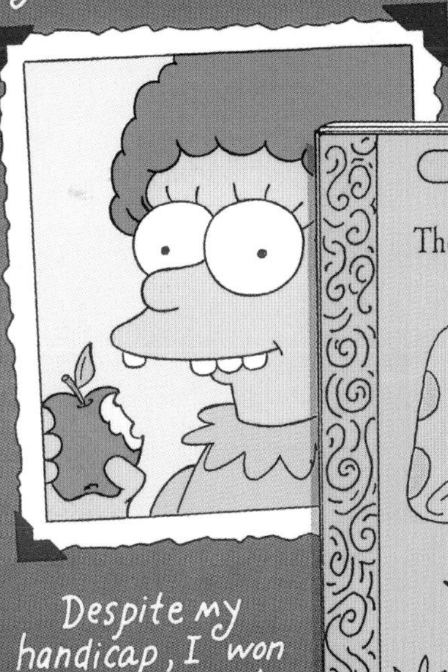

Despite my handicap, I won the kindergarten apple-bobbing contest.

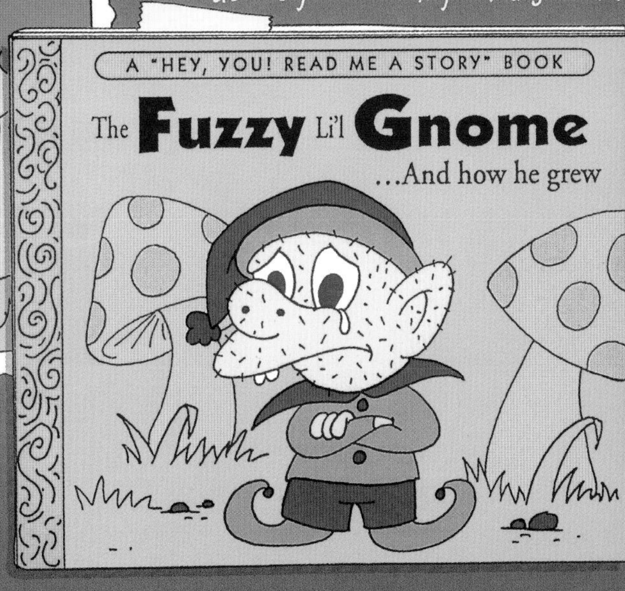
A "HEY, YOU! READ ME A STORY" BOOK
The Fuzzy Li'l Gnome
...And how he grew

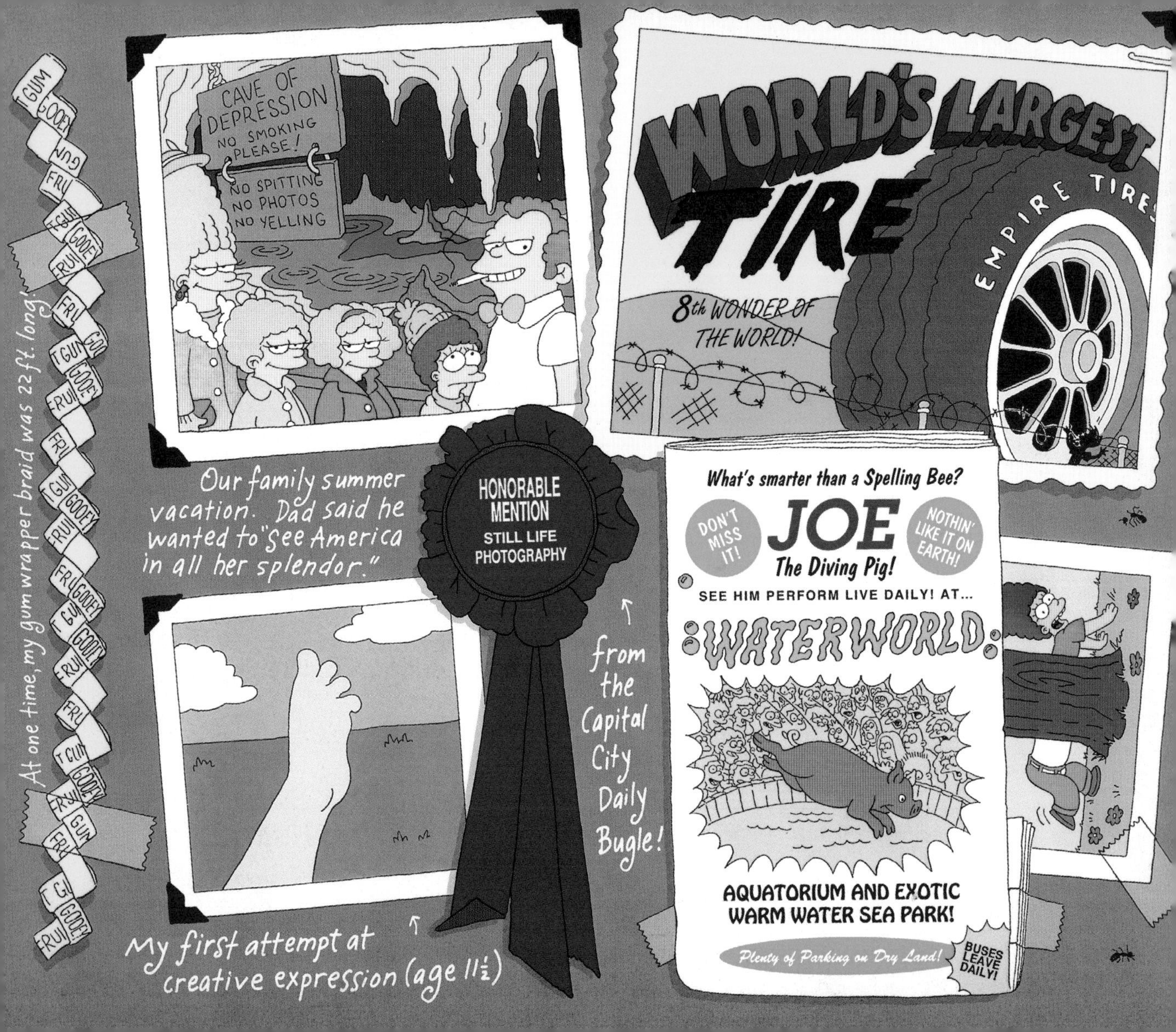
At one time, my gum wrapper braid was 22 ft. long!
CAVE OF DEPRESSION
NO SMOKING PLEASE!
NO SPITTING
NO PHOTOS
NO YELLING
WORLD'S LARGEST TIRE
8th WONDER OF THE WORLD!
EMPIRE TIRES
Our family summer vacation. Dad said he wanted to "See America in all her splendor."
HONORABLE MENTION
STILL LIFE PHOTOGRAPHY
from the Capital City Daily Bugle!
What's smarter than a Spelling Bee?
DON'T MISS IT!
JOE
The Diving Pig!
NOTHIN' LIKE IT ON EARTH!
SEE HIM PERFORM LIVE DAILY! AT...
WATERWORLD
AQUATORIUM AND EXOTIC WARM WATER SEA PARK!
Plenty of Parking on Dry Land!
BUSES LEAVE DAILY!
My first attempt at creative expression (age 11½)

Before ↓

After ↓

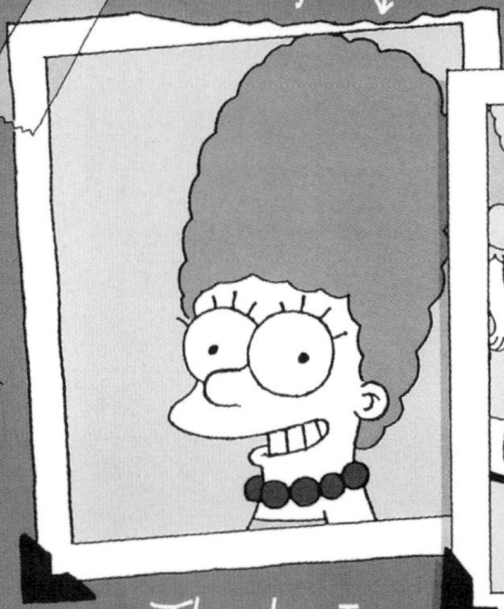

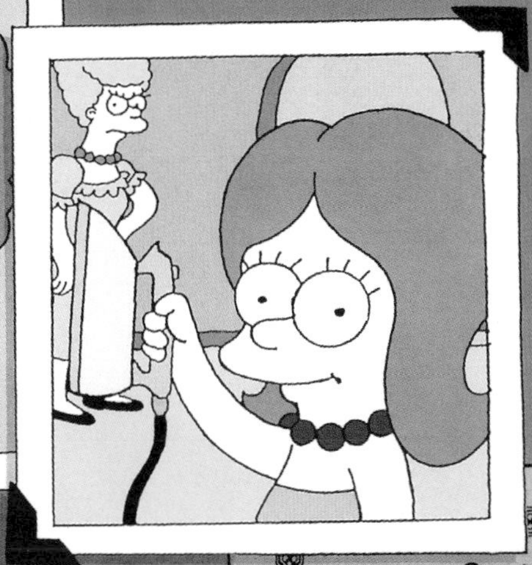

The day I straightened my hair (age 13).

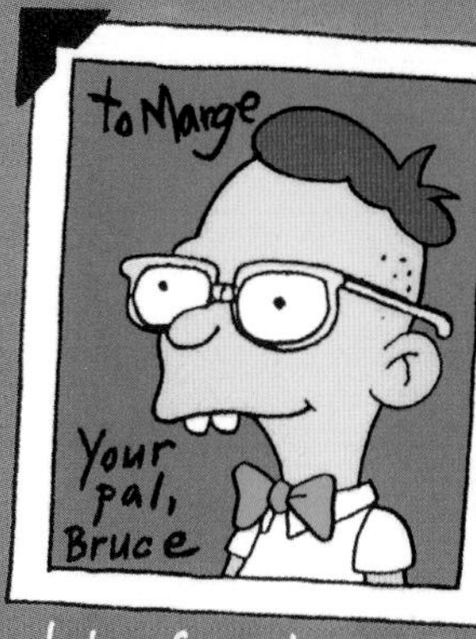
to Marge
Your pal, Bruce

My first boyfriend, Bruce Udelhofen

The Speech I Imagine JFK Would Have Made
At Our Graduation (Had H e Lived)

My fellow citizens of Springfield High, the trumpet summons us again toa long twilight struggle. THe torch has been passed to your generation and the glowfrom that fire can truly light the campus.

So let us Begin.

Ich bin ein Springfielder!

~~AXXMXXMK~~ Ask not what you can do for Springfield High, but what Springfield High can do for you..

Other way around?

The first draft of my award-winning dramatic interpretation

# Springfield High School

*Certificate of Distinction*

*Awarded to:* Marge Bouvier

*In recognition of:* "Johnny, We Hardly Heard Ye"

*In the Category:* Dramatic Interpretation

**2nd Place**

FORENSICS TEAM

Christina Marcello
Supervisor, Springfield School District

Seymour Skinner
Principal, Springfield High School

Artie Ziff took first place with his poignant reading of "Don't Rain on My Parade", from "Funny Girl."

# Grandpa Simpson's Army Days

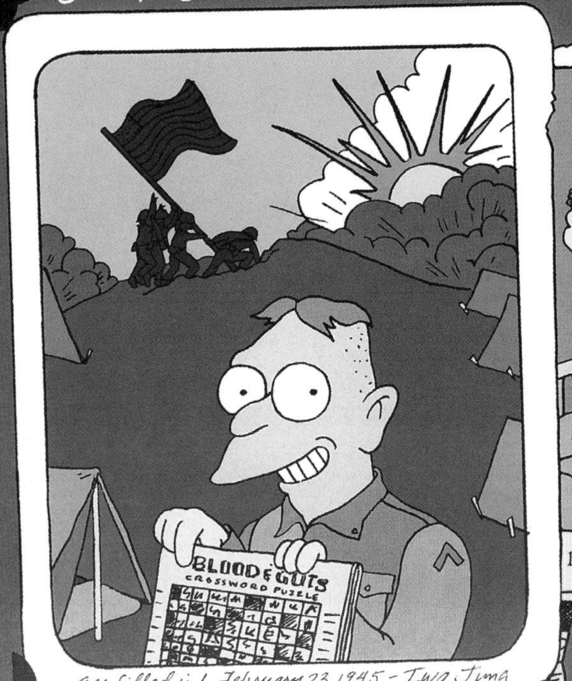
BLOOD & GUTS
CROSSWORD PUZZLE

All filled in! February 23, 1945 - Iwo Jima

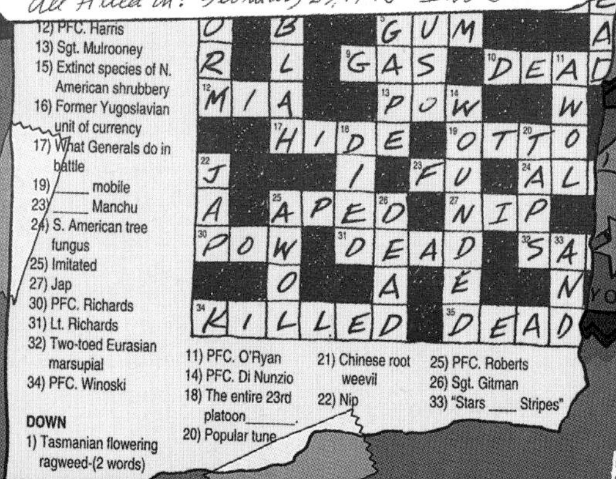
12) PFC. Harris
13) Sgt. Mulrooney
15) Extinct species of N. American shrubbery
16) Former Yugoslavian unit of currency
17) What Generals do in battle
19) _____ mobile
23) _____ Manchu
24) S. American tree fungus
25) Imitated
27) Jap
30) PFC. Richards
31) Lt. Richards
32) Two-toed Eurasian marsupial
34) PFC. Winoski

**DOWN**

1) Tasmanian flowering ragweed-(2 words)
11) PFC. O'Ryan
14) PFC. Di Nunzio
18) The entire 23rd platoon_______.
20) Popular tune
21) Chinese root weevil
22) Nip
25) PFC. Roberts
26) Sgt. Gitman
33) "Stars ____ Stripes"

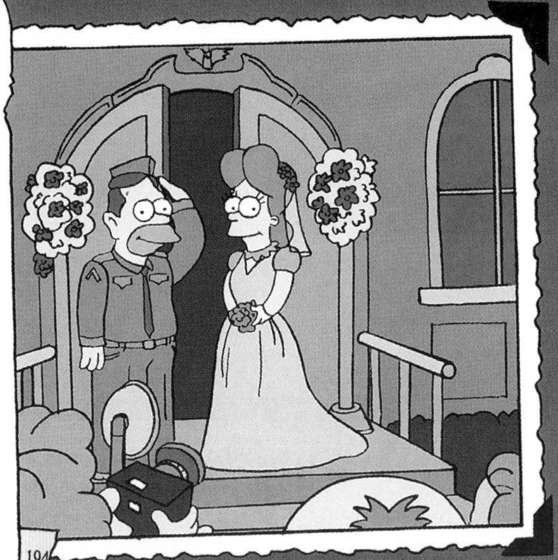

Grandma and Grandpa Simpson's wedding. I have them to thank for my dear Homer.

I found this in an old Almanac that Grandpa left in the bathroom.

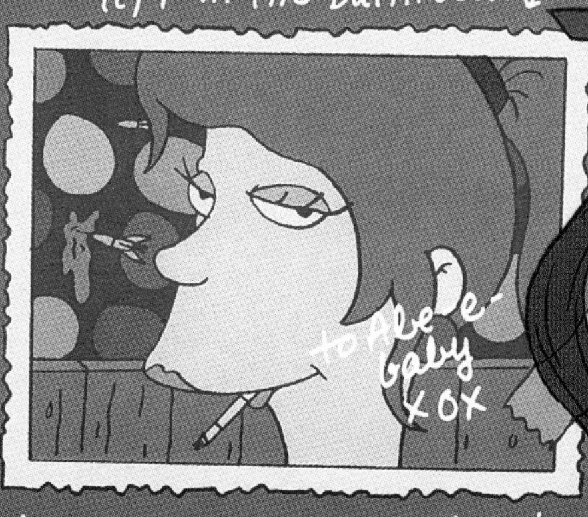
to Abe - Gaby
XOX

I don't know what her name was, but I do know that Homer's once-wealthy half-brother, Herb, was the result of their short-lived affair.

Springfield Shopper
314 Dutch Elm St.
Springfield

Dear Shopper Editor,

I~~'ve~~ have had it up to here with your "news-
paper" and it's reckless, anti-social policy
of publishing story afterstory of babies
being born, picture after picture of babies,
advertisements of baby products, etc.

Where will it all end?

What about the rest of us who are~~n't~~ not babies?
Did it ever occur to you that we are the
majority? If you ask me, you are only getting
yourself in a real mess because the people
will see all these babby stories and think
"That's a good way to get my name in the
paper," and that only leads to more babies!

So I'm ~~ware~~ warning you: if you continue this
policy, I will see to it that no child of
mine ever lays an eye on your publication.

Sicnerely,

*Abraham Simpson*

Abraham Simpson

P.S. If you don't think I'm serious, you
should see my newborn son. He shows no
interest in what your paper, or anything else
for that matter, has to say. More power to
him if you ask me!

Grandpa's first-recorded letter of complaint

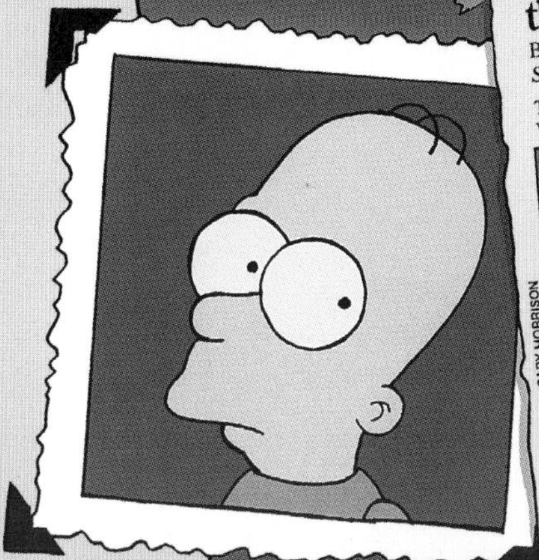

Little Homer Simpson, age 3 months

Grandpa's 7,587th oyster ↓

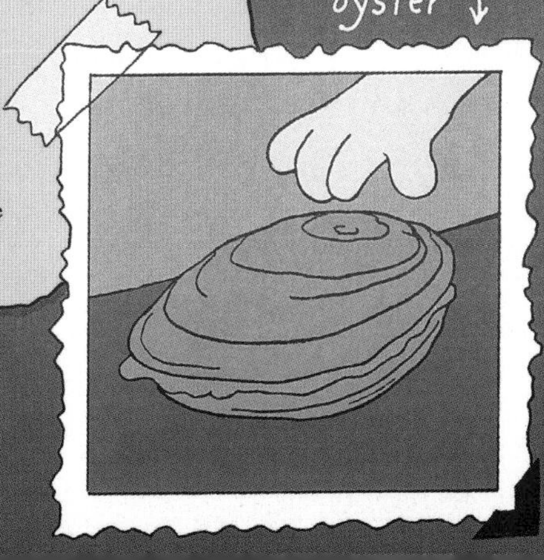

# SHUCKS, He's the World's Best!

By Merl Merlow,
*Shopper Business Editor*

The Springfield Oyster Shucking Co. was all abuzz Friday with the news that

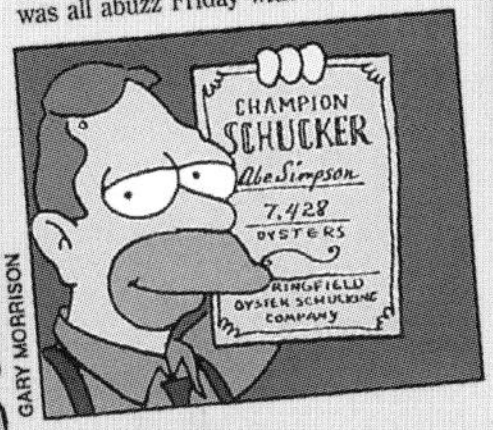
CHAMPION
SCHUCKER
Abe Simpson
7,428
OYSTERS
SPRINGFIELD
OYSTER SCHUCKING
COMPANY
GARY MORRISON

**Abe Simpson**

Abraham Simpson, 29, had hand-shucked 7,587 oysters between 8:00 Monday morning and 5:00 Friday afternoon.

Simpson's achievement surpassed the previous one-week record of 7,428, set by the late Lud "Load" Dennison in 1943.

"Not to take anything away from Lud or his beautiful widow," said an elated Abe Simpson when presented with a handsome scroll commemorating his feat, "but you have to remember that the Load set the record in a six-day work week during the war, when the only thing this place turned out was beef in a tin.

"I'd like to see [Dennison] try to break 5,000, let alone come close to my record, with big jumbos and those pretty little ones sailing down the conveyor belt. Now *that's* shuckin'."

Simpson said he planned to celebrate quietly at home with his 3-month-old son Homer.

"I'll probably just relax in front of the radio and try to get the smell off my hands," Simpson said.

In other business news... C. Montgomery Burns, 23, purchased the run down Springfield Gas and Electric Co., which has been closed for the past

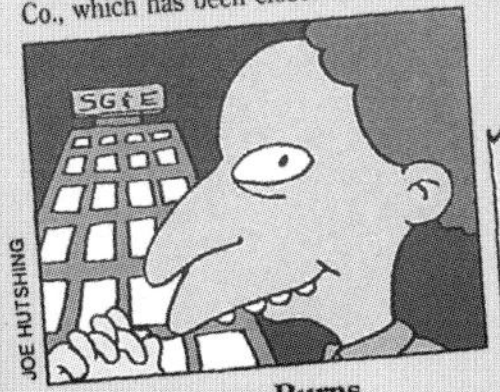
SG&E
JOE HUTSHING

**C. Montgomery Burns**

five weeks. When asked whether he would reinstate the "Lights Out for the Weekend" campaign, Burns said, "By the time I'm through, there'll be enough power around here to light up four or five Springfields!"

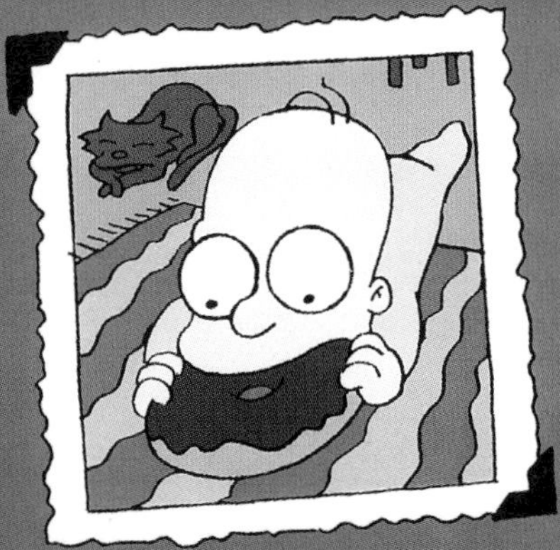

Homer always did have a fondness for donuts.

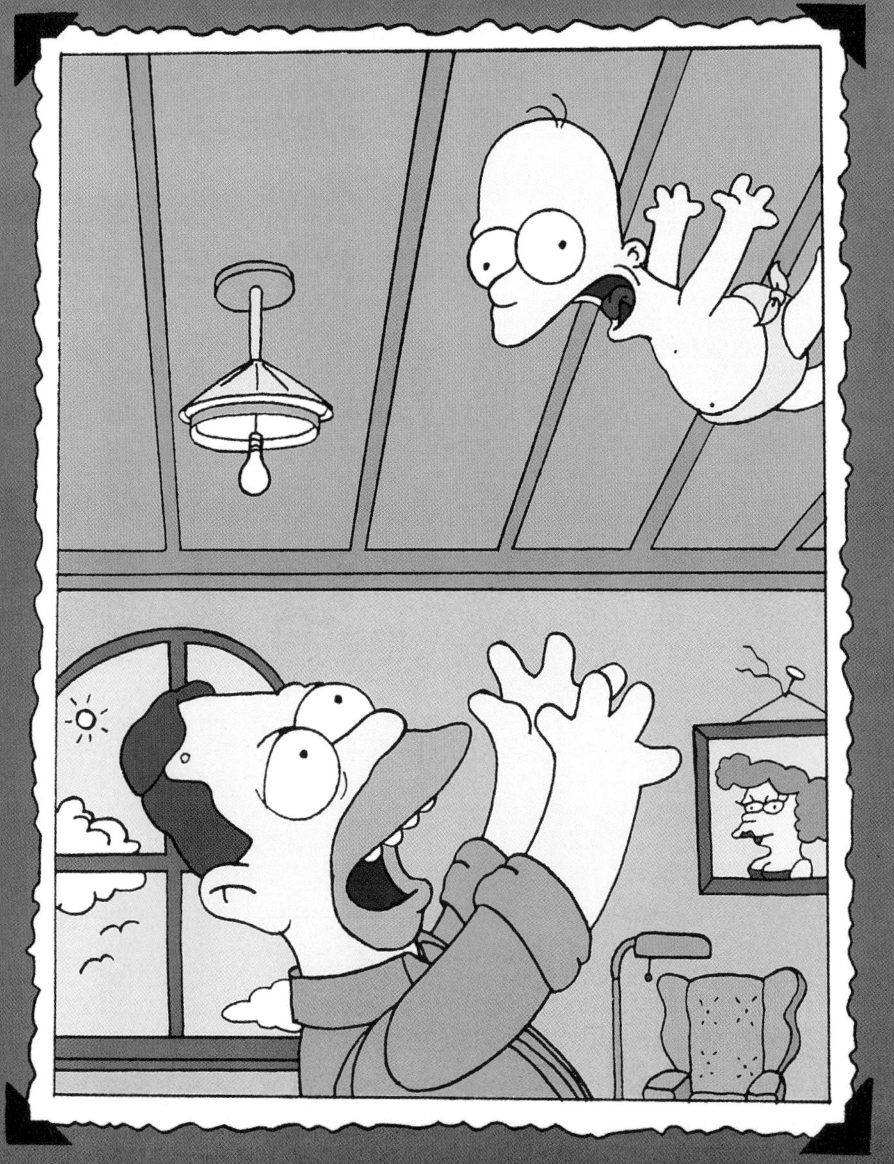

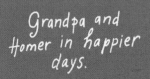

Grandpa and Homer in happier days.

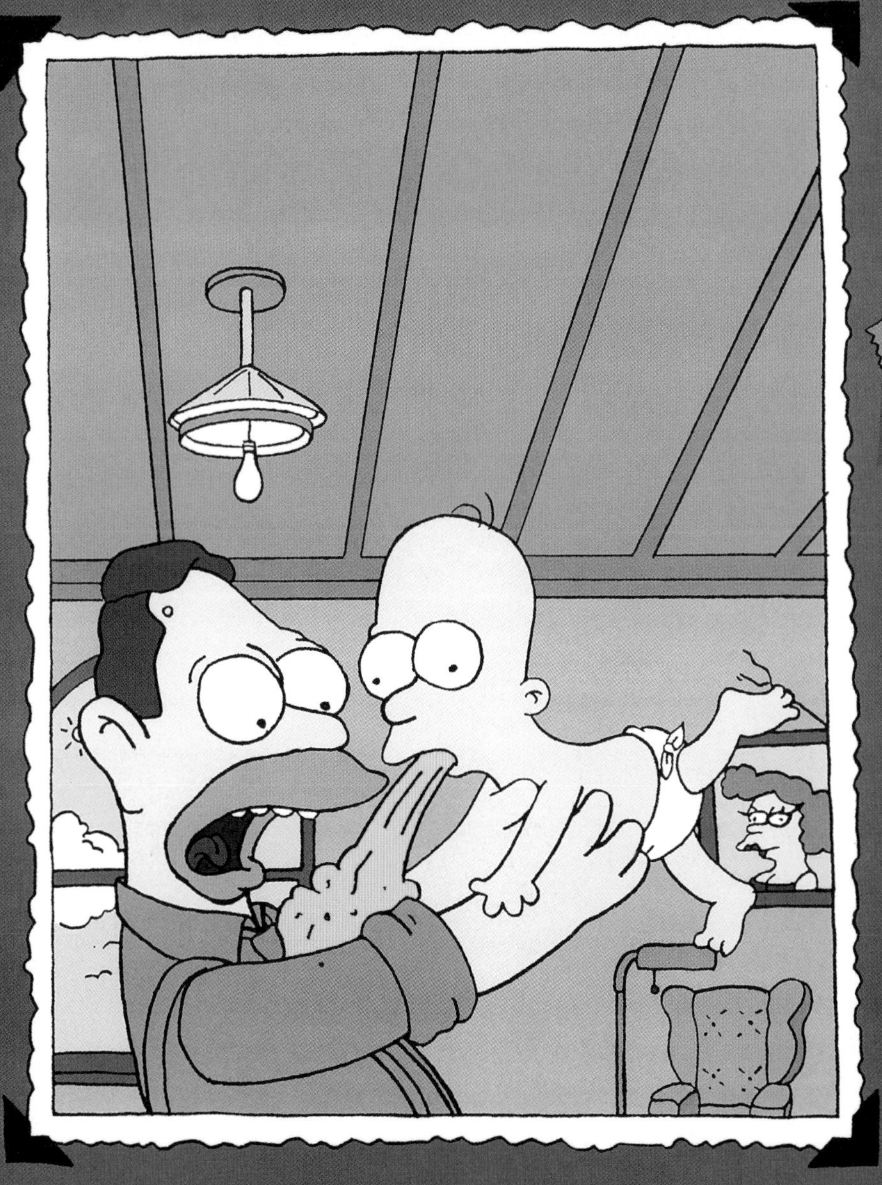

The first sign of Homer's budding intelligence. I can't really say his handwriting has improved much over the years.

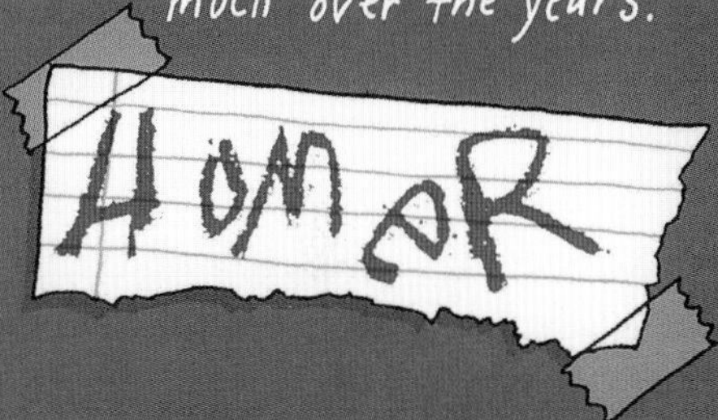
HOMeR

The happier days were over quite quickly.

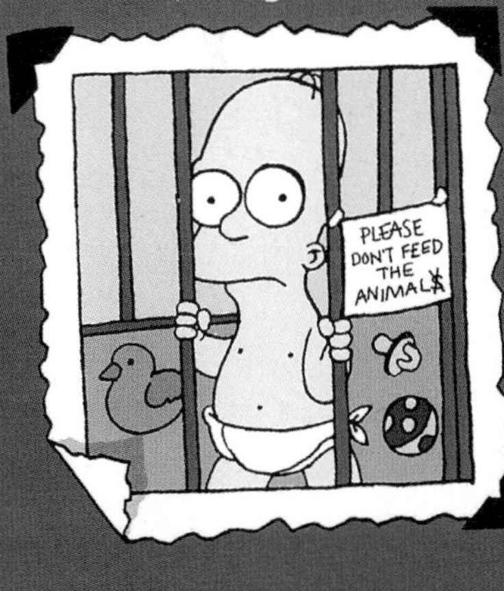
PLEASE DON'T FEED THE ANIMAL$

**SPRINGFIELD ELEMENTARY**

*"We mold young minds."*
--Douglas Crone, Ed D., Superintendent

SPRINGFIELD
Est. 1914

REPORT CARD

~~Simpson, Homer~~ GRADE 4

| SUBJECT | 1ST QUARTER | 2ND QUARTER | 3RD QUARTER | 4TH QUARTER | SUMMER-SCHOOL |
|---|---|---|---|---|---|
| MATH | D | D | D- | D- | F |
| ENG | D+ | D | D- | F+ | F |
| HIST | D | D+ | D+ | D- | F |
| SCI | D- | D- | F | D- | F |
| GYM | C- | C- | D | D+ | D- |
| ATTEN-DANCE | F | D- | F | D- | F |
| CITIZEN-SHIP | F | D- | D- | F | D- |

**NOTES** ~~we would like to hold Homer back a year, but his 4th grade teacher, Mrs. Harvell, has refused to take him back —HH~~

an insult to ... disruption

"underachiel

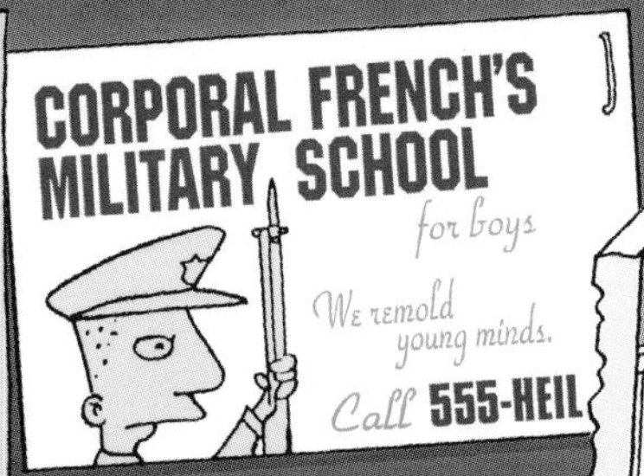
CORPORAL FRENCH'S MILITARY SCHOOL
for boys
We remold young minds.
Call 555-HEIL

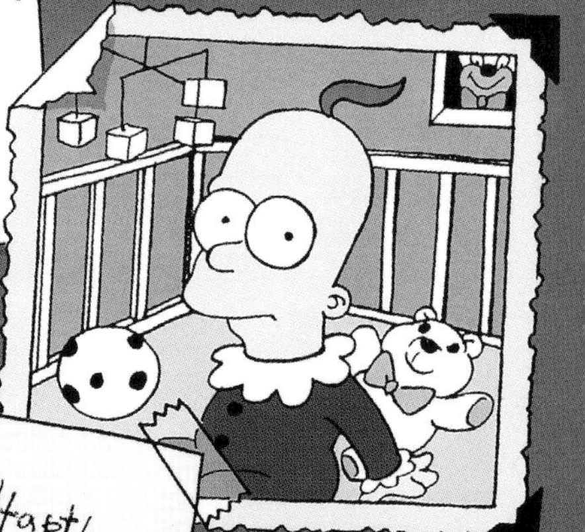

Our only photo of Herb Powell, Homer's once-wealthy half-brother.

Dear Principal Hartly,
Please excuse Homer's absince of Nov. 8-10. He had to stay home to look after his fathre, who was nearly blinded when he reached to a high shelf and took down a bottle of cleanser he wus going to use to clean his medal for the Veterins Day Parade and the cleansr spilled in his face.
Signed,
HOMER'S DAD

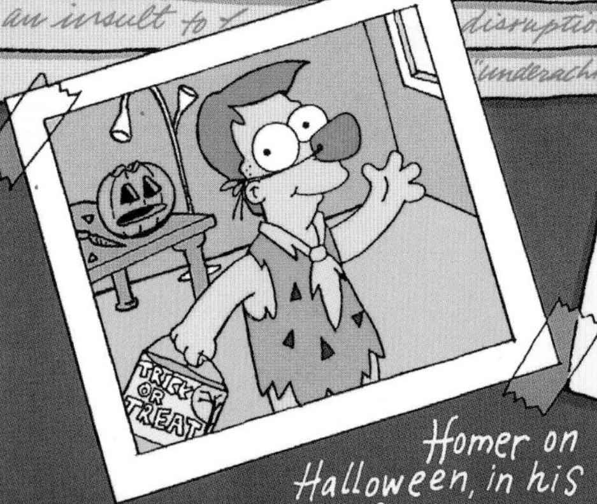
TRICK OR TREAT

Homer on Halloween, in his all-time favorite costume. (age four)

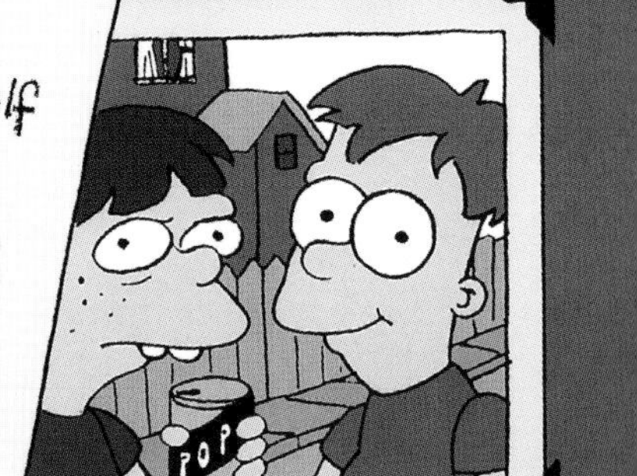
POP

Homer at the tender age of ten. That's Barney Gumble on the left.

Dear Dad,
I'll do anything you say, just don't send me to military schoul. Please please please please please please please please please please.
Your devotid son,
Homer

P.S. Remember. Today is the first day of the rest of your life.

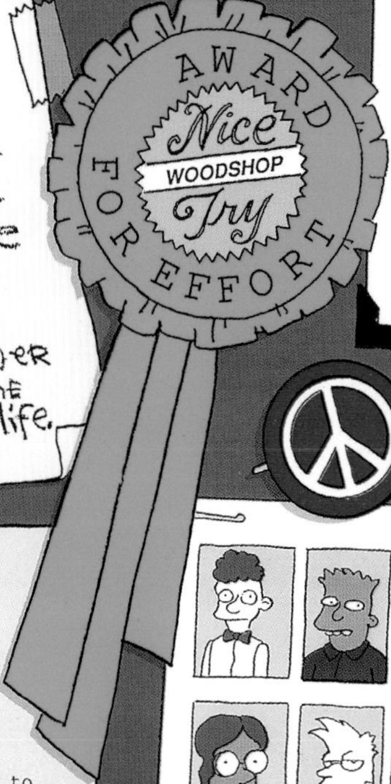
AWARD FOR EFFORT
Nice
WOODSHOP
Try

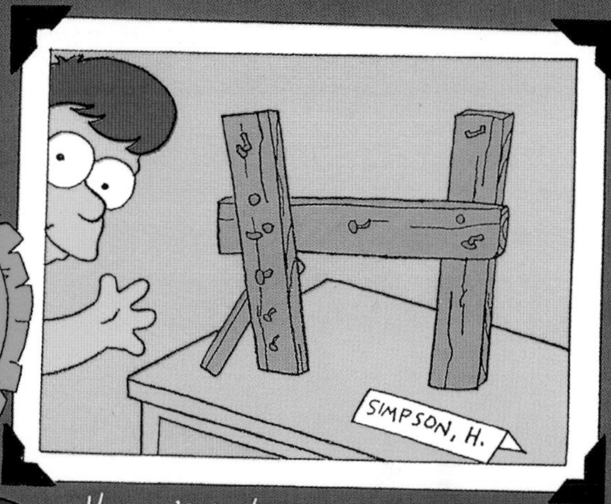
SIMPSON, H.

Homer's sophomore woodshop project - his first initial. He planned to finish the "J" as a junior and the "S" as a senior.

FROM THE DESK OF

**Harlan Dondelinger**

To: Abraham Simpson

From: Harlan Dondelinger
Vice Principal

Dear Mr. Simpson:

I need to talk with you about ways to improve Homer's study habits. His constant efforts to draw attention to himself with noises imitating bodily functions and his off-color attempts at humor during class time have reached the point where I have no alternative but to warn you that drastic measures may be necessary. We've told him repeatedly that he's an underachiever, but Homer seems to think that's a compliment.

Sincerely,

Harlan Dondelinger
Vice Principal

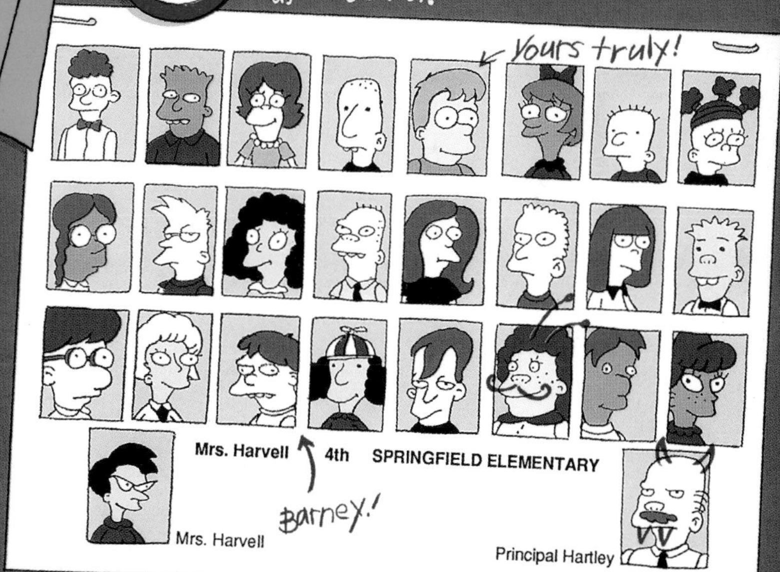
Yours truly!
Mrs. Harvell
4th
SPRINGFIELD ELEMENTARY
Barney!
Mrs. Harvell
Principal Hartley

On prom night I wore my hair UP for the first time! A style that's never let me DOWN.

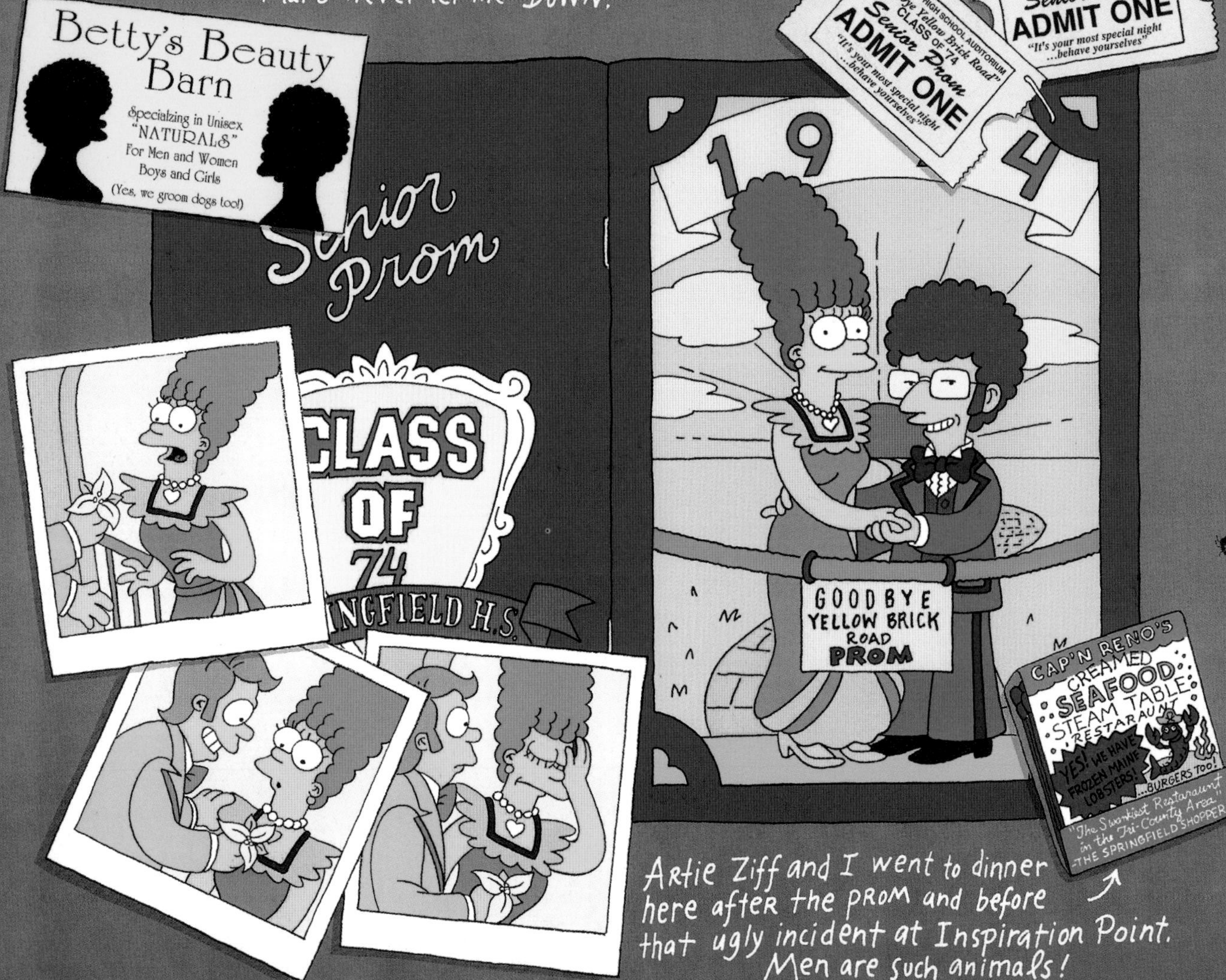
Betty's Beauty Barn
Specialzing in Unisex "NATURALS" For Men and Women Boys and Girls
(Yes, we groom dogs too!)
SPRINGFIELD HIGH SCHOOL AUDITORIUM
"Goodbye Yellow Brick Road"
CLASS OF '74
Senior Prom
ADMIT ONE
"It's your most special night ...behave yourselves"
SPRINGFIELD HIGH SCHOOL AUDITORIUM
"Goodbye Yellow Brick Road"
CLASS OF '74
Senior Prom
ADMIT ONE
"It's your most special night ...behave yourselves"
Senior Prom
CLASS OF 74
INGFIELD H.S.
1 9 4
GOODBYE YELLOW BRICK ROAD PROM
CAP'N RENO'S
CREAMED SEAFOOD STEAM TABLE RESTARAUNT
YES! WE HAVE FROZEN MAINE LOBSTERS!
...BURGERS TOO!
"The Swankiest Restaraunt in the Tri-County Area." -THE SPRINGFIELD SHOPPER

Artie Ziff and I went to dinner here after the PROM and before that ugly incident at Inspiration Point. Men are such animals!

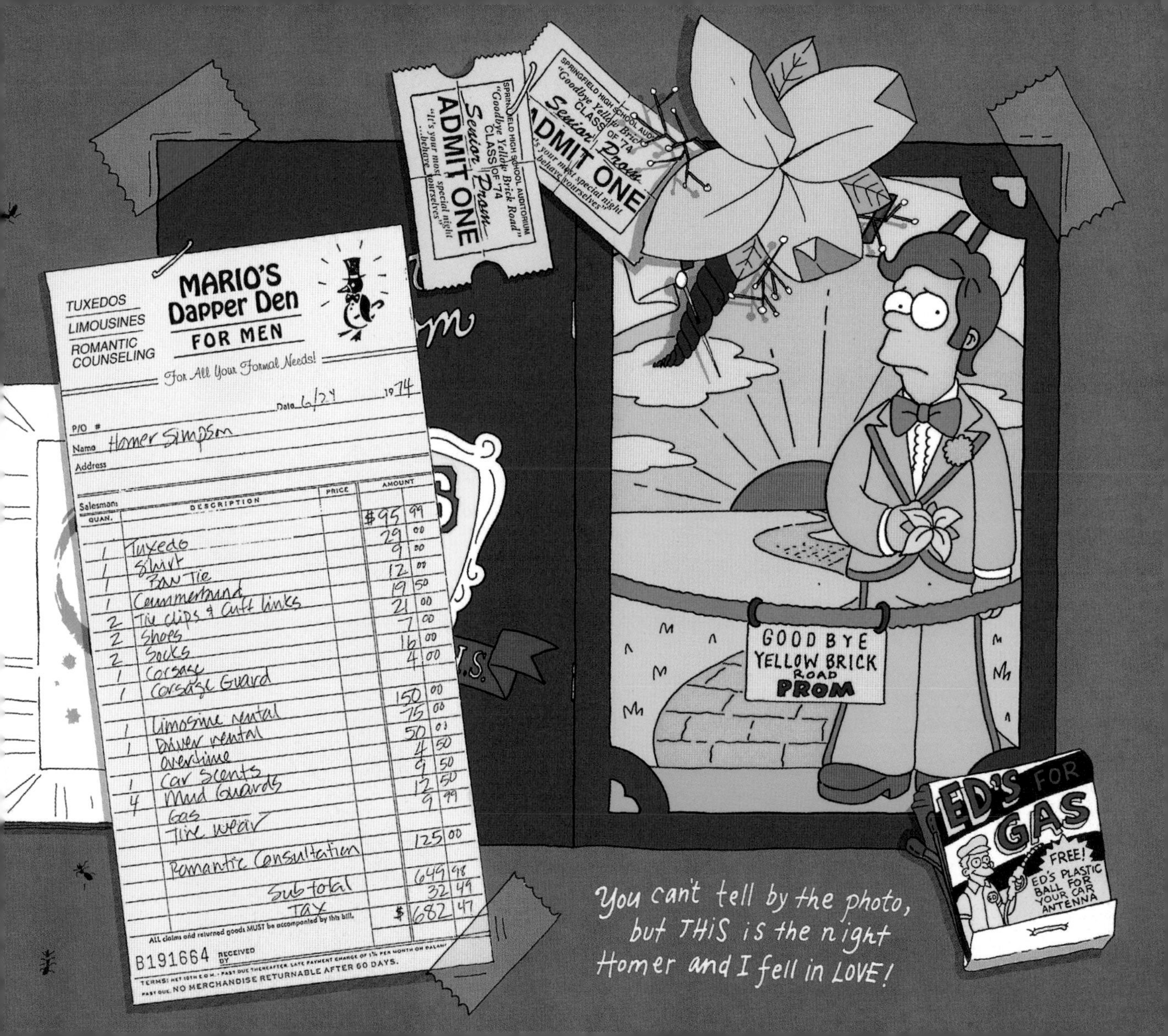

MARIO'S Dapper Den FOR MEN
TUXEDOS
LIMOUSINES
ROMANTIC COUNSELING
For All Your Formal Needs!
Date 6/24 1974
P/O #
Name Homer Simpson
Address
Salesman:
QUAN. DESCRIPTION PRICE AMOUNT
1 Tuxedo $95 99
1 Shirt 29 00
1 Bow Tie 9 00
1 Cummerbund 12 00
2 Tie clips & Cuff links 19 50
2 Shoes 21 00
2 Socks 7 00
1 Corsage 16 00
1 Corsage Guard 4 00
1 Limosine rental 150 00
1 Driver rental 75 00
overtime 50 00
1 Car Scents 4 50
4 Mud Guards 9 50
Gas 12 50
Tire wear 9 99
Romantic Consultation 125 00
Sub total 649 98
Tax 32 49
$ 682 47
ALL claims and returned goods MUST be accompanied by this bill.
B191664 RECEIVED BY
NO MERCHANDISE RETURNABLE AFTER 60 DAYS.
SPRINGFIELD HIGH SCHOOL AUDITORIUM
"Goodbye Yellow Brick Road"
CLASS OF '74
Senior Prom
ADMIT ONE
"it's your most special night ...behave yourselves"
GOODBYE YELLOW BRICK ROAD PROM
ED'S FOR GAS
FREE! ED'S PLASTIC BALL FOR YOUR CAR ANTENNA
You can't tell by the photo, but THIS is the night Homer and I fell in LOVE!

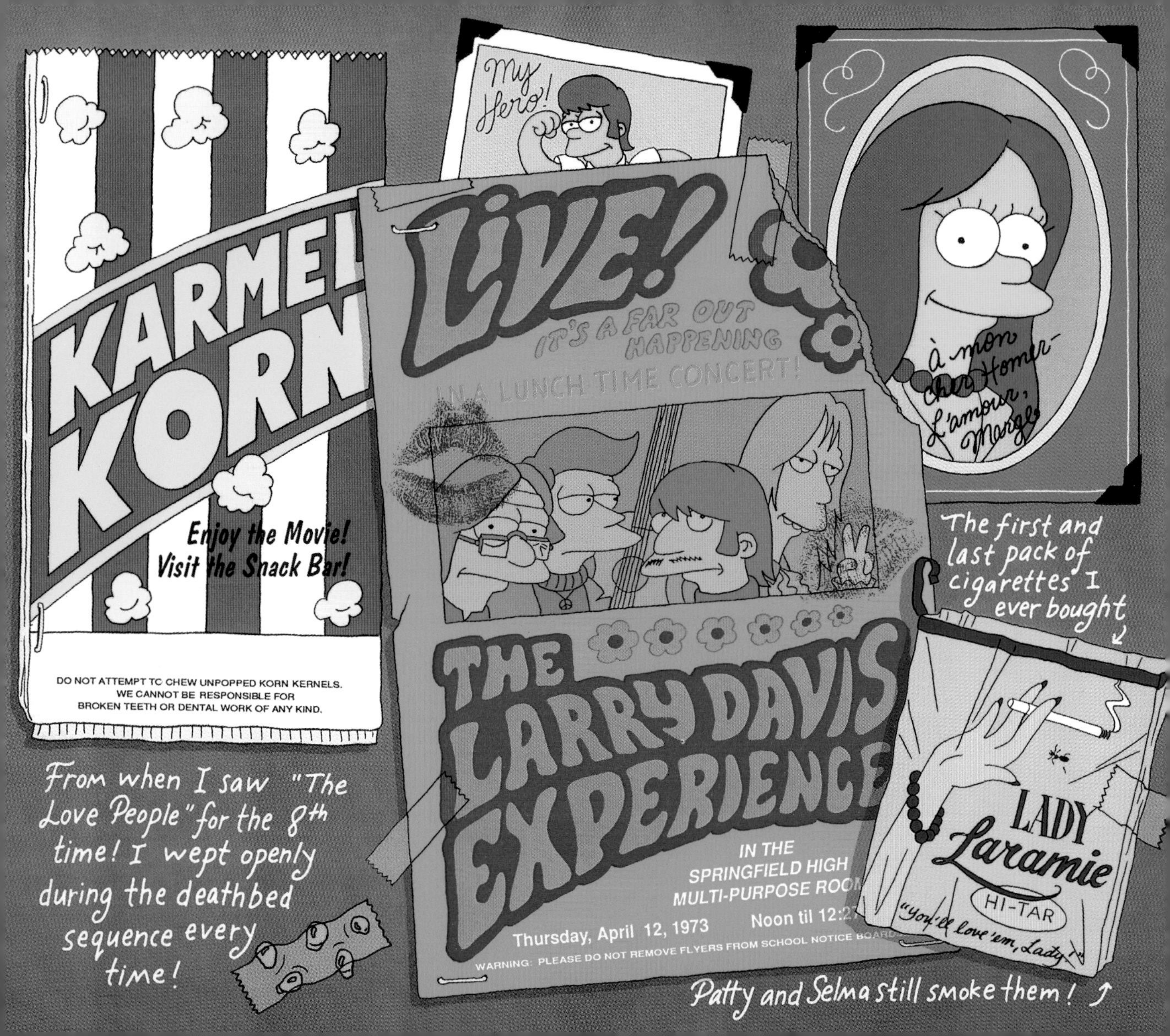
KARMEL KORN
Enjoy the Movie! Visit the Snack Bar!
DO NOT ATTEMPT TC CHEW UNPOPPED KORN KERNELS. WE CANNOT BE RESPONSIBLE FOR BROKEN TEETH OR DENTAL WORK OF ANY KIND.
From when I saw "The Love People" for the 8th time! I wept openly during the deathbed sequence every time!
My Hero!
LIVE!
IT'S A FAR OUT HAPPENING
IN A LUNCH TIME CONCERT!
THE LARRY DAVIS EXPERIENCE
IN THE SPRINGFIELD HIGH MULTI-PURPOSE ROO
Thursday, April 12, 1973
Noon til 12:2
WARNING: PLEASE DO NOT REMOVE FLYERS FROM SCHOOL NOTICE BOAR
À mon cher Homer – L'amour, Marge
The first and last pack of cigarettes I ever bought
LADY Laramie
HI-TAR
"You'll love 'em, Lady!"
Patty and Selma still smoke them!

# HANDWRITING ANALYSIS

## *Your* Personality Revealed Through Penmanship!

SIGNATURE *Marge Bouvier*

Your signature indicates a sensitive, free-spirited and creative nature. The graceful calligraphic curvatures of your capital letters reveal a love of poetry and music. You are destined for a life of elegance, refinement and artistic fulfillment.

SIGNATURE **HOMER SIMPSON**

Your signature exhibits a strong tendency toward slackness, inattention and woolgathering. The unsophisticated arrangement of ill-formed lines and circles which comprise your writing suggests an obtuse and insipid outlook. You are doomed to a life of banality, dullness and lethargy.

ROSES ARE RED
Violets ARE
BLUE NO ONE
I KNOW
speaks French
As Beautifully
As you,
L'Amour,
HOMER

My 10 favorite Bands of All time, 1973

1. Ringo Starr
2. The Beatles
3. The Larry Davis Experience
4. The Happies
5. Elf Gravy
6. Don Donnally and Jo-Jo
7. Beatlemania
8. The Twigs of Sister Tomorrow
9. The Love Buckets
10. Mr. Funky and the Springfieldians

*R.S. + M.B.*

Homer's other love — his car
Such fond memories!

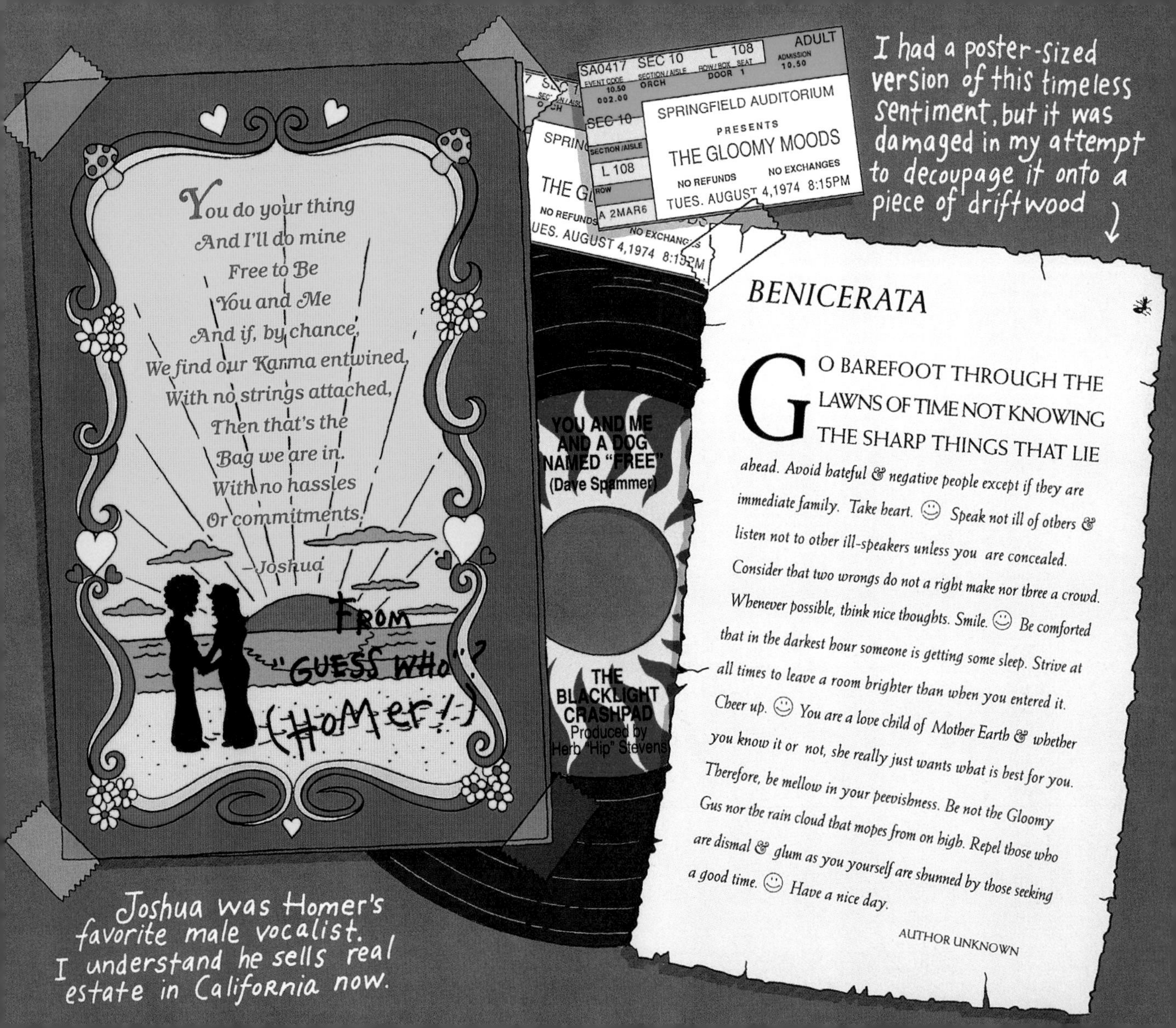
You do your thing
And I'll do mine
Free to Be
You and Me
And if, by chance,
We find our Karma entwined,
With no strings attached,
Then that's the
Bag we are in.
With no hassles
Or commitments.
—Joshua
FROM
"GUESS WHO"?
(HOMER!)
SA0417 SEC 10 L 108 ADULT
EVENT CODE SECTION / AISLE ROW / BOX SEAT ADMISSION
10.50 ORCH DOOR 1 10.50
002.00
SEC 10
SECTION / AISLE
L 108
ROW
A 2MAR6
SPRINGFIELD AUDITORIUM
PRESENTS
THE GLOOMY MOODS
NO REFUNDS NO EXCHANGES
TUES. AUGUST 4,1974 8:15PM
I had a poster-sized version of this timeless sentiment, but it was damaged in my attempt to decoupage it onto a piece of driftwood
YOU AND ME AND A DOG NAMED "FREE"
(Dave Spammer)
THE BLACKLIGHT CRASHPAD
Produced by Herb "Hip" Stevens
BENICERATA
GO BAREFOOT THROUGH THE LAWNS OF TIME NOT KNOWING THE SHARP THINGS THAT LIE ahead. Avoid hateful & negative people except if they are immediate family. Take heart. ☺ Speak not ill of others & listen not to other ill-speakers unless you are concealed. Consider that two wrongs do not a right make nor three a crowd. Whenever possible, think nice thoughts. Smile. ☺ Be comforted that in the darkest hour someone is getting some sleep. Strive at all times to leave a room brighter than when you entered it. Cheer up. ☺ You are a love child of Mother Earth & whether you know it or not, she really just wants what is best for you. Therefore, be mellow in your peevishness. Be not the Gloomy Gus nor the rain cloud that mopes from on high. Repel those who are dismal & glum as you yourself are shunned by those seeking a good time. ☺ Have a nice day.
AUTHOR UNKNOWN
Joshua was Homer's favorite male vocalist. I understand he sells real estate in California now.

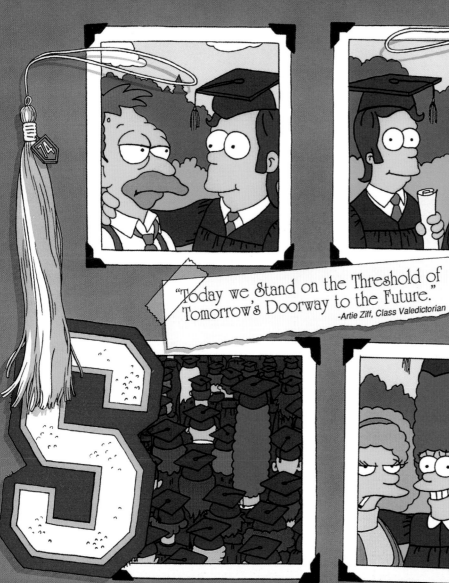

"Today we Stand on the Threshold of Tomorrow's Doorway to the Future."
-Artie Ziff, Class Valedictorian

"Les Bouvier Girls" (That's me in the middle!)

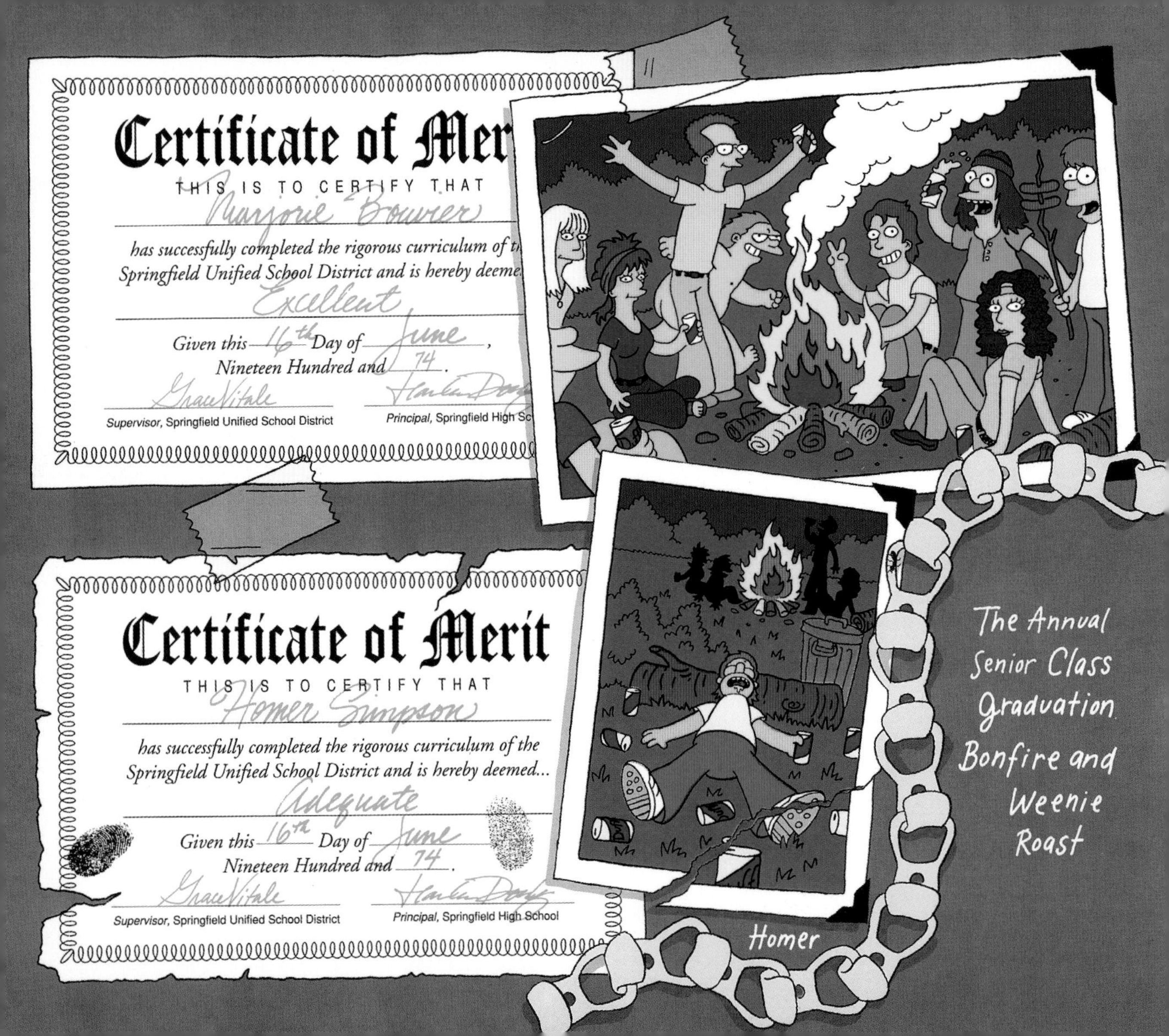
Certificate of Mer
THIS IS TO CERTIFY THAT
Marjorie Bouvier
has successfully completed the rigorous curriculum of t
Springfield Unified School District and is hereby deeme
Excellent
Given this 16th Day of June,
Nineteen Hundred and 74.
Grace Vitale
Supervisor, Springfield Unified School District
Principal, Springfield High Sc
Certificate of Merit
THIS IS TO CERTIFY THAT
Homer Simpson
has successfully completed the rigorous curriculum of the
Springfield Unified School District and is hereby deemed...
Adequate
Given this 16th Day of June
Nineteen Hundred and 74.
Grace Vitale
Supervisor, Springfield Unified School District
Principal, Springfield High School
Homer
The Annual Senior Class Graduation Bonfire and Weenie Roast

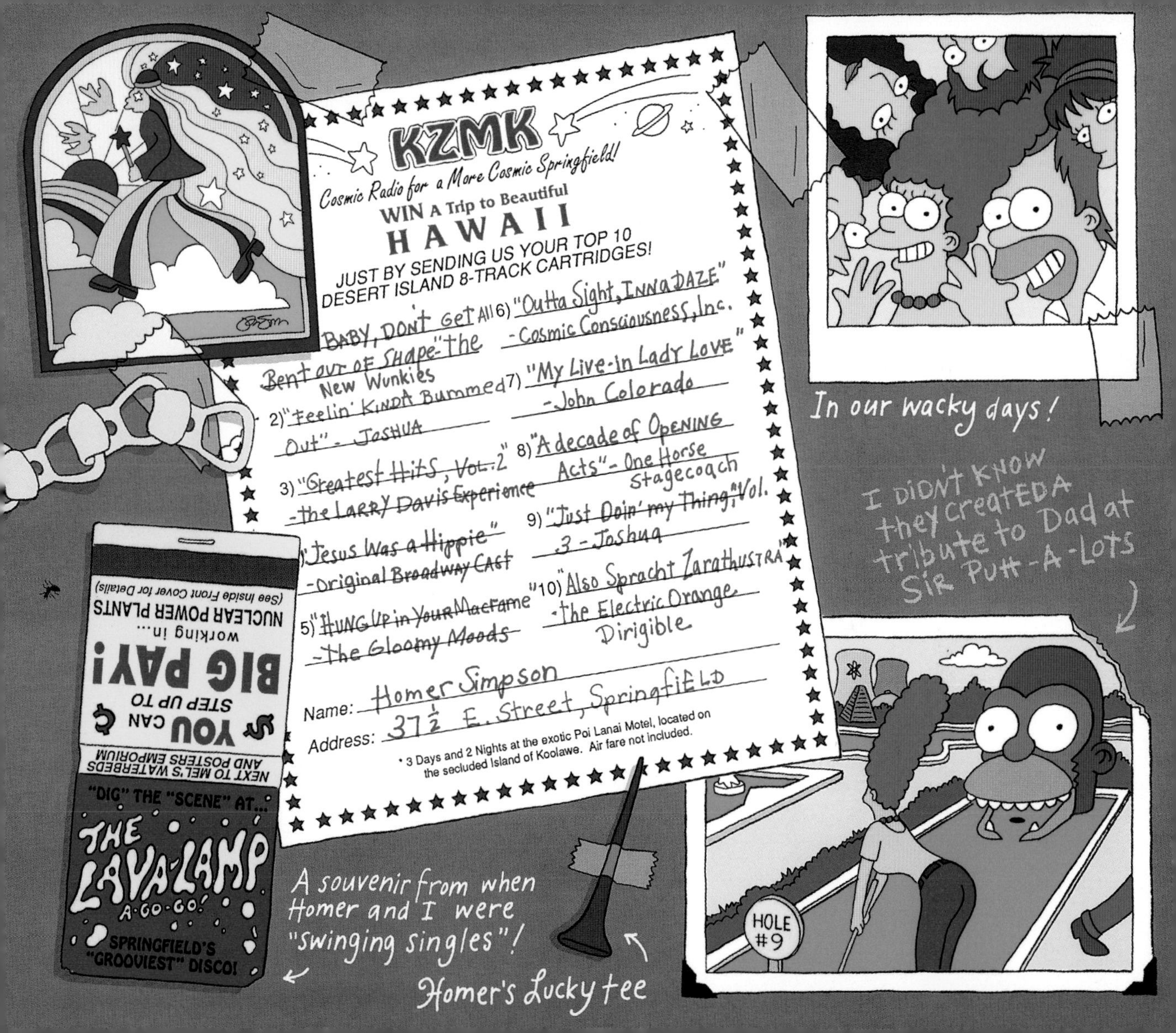

KZMK
Cosmic Radio for a More Cosmic Springfield!
WIN A Trip to Beautiful
HAWAII
JUST BY SENDING US YOUR TOP 10
DESERT ISLAND 8-TRACK CARTRIDGES!
"BABY, DON'T GET All Bent out of Shape" - the New Wunkies
2) "Feelin' KINDA Bummed Out" - JOSHUA
3) "Greatest Hits, Vol. 2" - the LARRY Davis Experience
"Jesus Was a Hippie" - Original Broadway CAST
5) "HUNG Up in Your Macrame" - The Gloomy Moods
6) "Outta Sight, INNA DAZE" - Cosmic Consciousness, Inc.
7) "My Live-in Lady Love" - John Colorado
8) "A decade of OPENING Acts" - One Horse Stagecoach
9) "Just Doin' my Thing," Vol. 3 - Joshua
10) "Also Spracht Zarathustra" - The Electric Orange Dirigible
Name: Homer Simpson
Address: 37½ E. Street, Springfield
* 3 Days and 2 Nights at the exotic Poi Lanai Motel, located on the secluded Island of Koolawe. Air fare not included.
In our wacky days!
I DIDN'T KNOW they created A tribute to Dad at Sir Putt-A-Lots
HOLE #9
(See Inside Front Cover for Details)
NUCLEAR POWER PLANTS
working in...
BIG PAY!
STEP UP TO
YOU CAN
NEXT TO MEL'S WATERBEDS AND POSTERS EMPORIUM
"DIG" THE "SCENE" AT...
THE LAVA-LAMP A-GO-GO!
SPRINGFIELD'S "GROOVIEST" DISCO!
A souvenir from when Homer and I were "swinging singles"!
Homer's Lucky tee

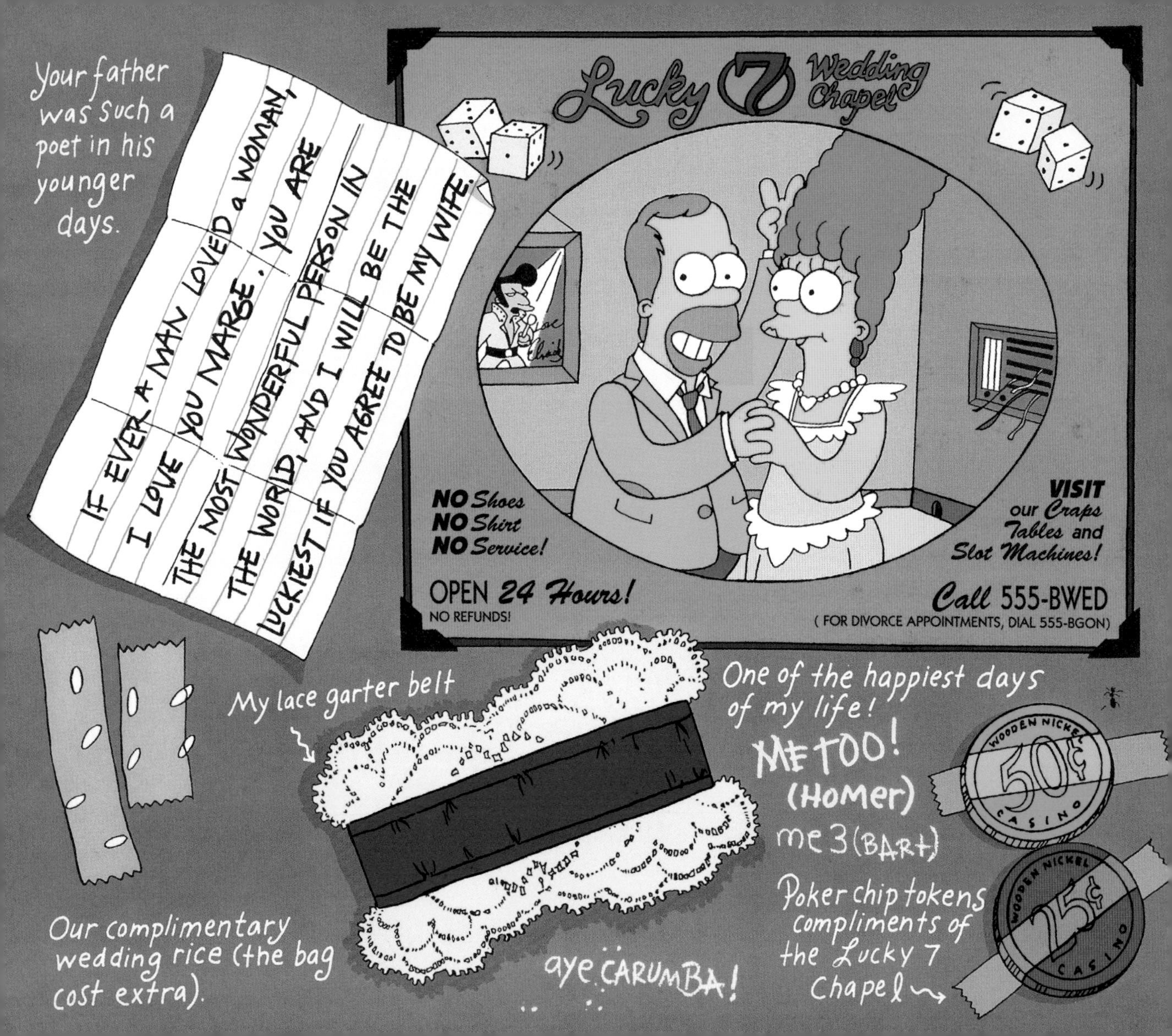
Your father was such a poet in his younger days.
IF EVER A MAN LOVED a WOMAN, I LOVE YOU MARGE. YOU ARE THE MOST WONDERFUL PERSON IN THE WORLD, AND I WILL BE THE LUCKIEST IF YOU AGREE TO BE MY WIFE.
Lucky 7 Wedding Chapel
NO Shoes
NO Shirt
NO Service!
VISIT our Craps Tables and Slot Machines!
OPEN 24 Hours!
NO REFUNDS!
Call 555-BWED
( FOR DIVORCE APPOINTMENTS, DIAL 555-BGON)
My lace garter belt
One of the happiest days of my life!
ME TOO!
(HOMER)
me 3 (BART)
WOODEN NICKEL 50¢ CASINO
WOODEN NICKEL 25¢ CASINO
Poker chip tokens compliments of the Lucky 7 Chapel
Our complimentary wedding rice (the bag cost extra).
aye CARUMBA!

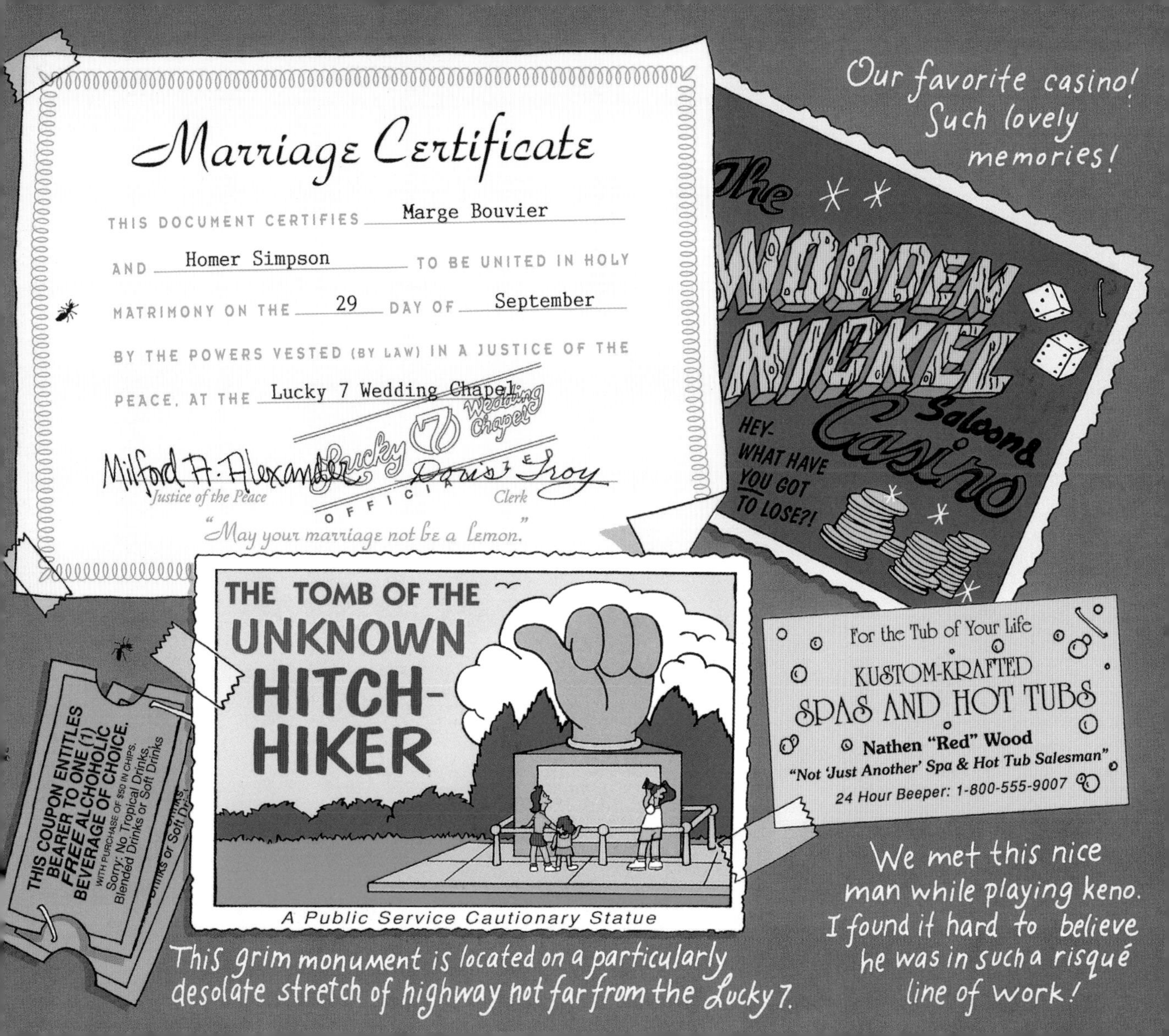
Marriage Certificate
THIS DOCUMENT CERTIFIES Marge Bouvier
AND Homer Simpson TO BE UNITED IN HOLY
MATRIMONY ON THE 29 DAY OF September
BY THE POWERS VESTED (BY LAW) IN A JUSTICE OF THE
PEACE, AT THE Lucky 7 Wedding Chapel
Lucky 7 Wedding Chapel OFFICIAL
Milford A. Alexander
Justice of the Peace
Doris Troy
Clerk
"May your marriage not be a lemon."
Our favorite casino! Such lovely memories!
The Wooden Nickel Saloon & Casino
HEY- WHAT HAVE YOU GOT TO LOSE?!
THE TOMB OF THE UNKNOWN HITCH-HIKER
A Public Service Cautionary Statue
This grim monument is located on a particularly desolate stretch of highway not far from the Lucky 7.
THIS COUPON ENTITLES BEARER TO ONE (1) FREE ALCHOHOLIC BEVERAGE OF CHOICE.
WITH PURCHASE OF $50 IN CHIPS.
Sorry: No Tropical Drinks, Blended Drinks or Soft Drinks
For the Tub of Your Life
KUSTOM-KRAFTED
SPAS AND HOT TUBS
Nathen "Red" Wood
"Not 'Just Another' Spa & Hot Tub Salesman"
24 Hour Beeper: 1-800-555-9007
We met this nice man while playing keno. I found it hard to believe he was in such a risqué line of work!

DEAR Ringo,

I hope you like this paINTING I DID of you. You are my favorite musician in the universe (really!)

What do you like to eat?
Is your hair really that shape all the time?
Do you have hamburgers and French fries in England?

Well, that's all for now. Please write me you have time in your very busy schedule.

Yours truly,

Your biggest fan,

Marge Bouvier :)

Marge Bouvier

(P.S. I am not a lunatic.)

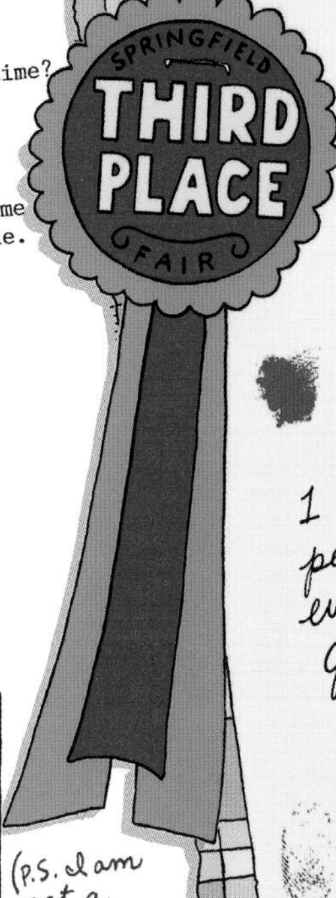
SPRINGFIELD
THIRD PLACE
FAIR

# Lucky Coin Gelatin Mold

(Whoever gets the coin is Lucky for a day!)

2 packs blue gelatin mix

3 cups "Krusty Brand" corn sweetener

1 lb. bag multi-colored "Kitchen Dee-Lite" miniature marshmallows

1 Lucky coin (for chefs on a budget, pennies are acceptable. For special events, try using a Bicentennial quarter.)

My secret ingredient:

Fla

Boil gelatin i
Pour into m
Add marshm
Chill for

Voila!

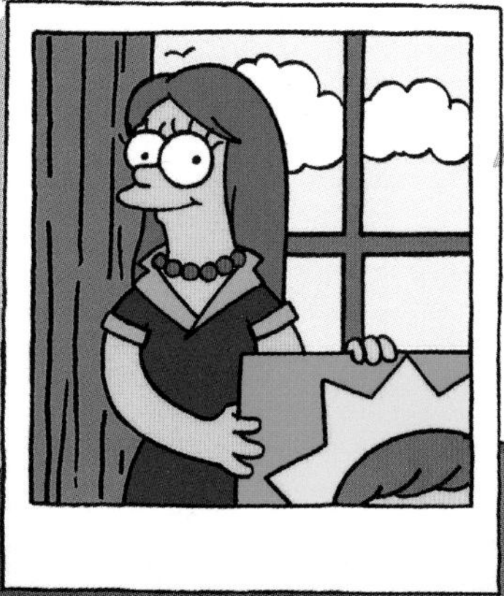

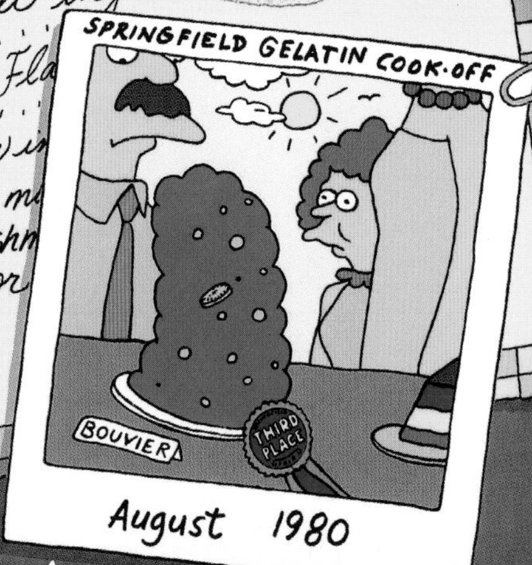
SPRINGFIELD GELATIN COOK-OFF
BOUVIER
THIRD PLACE

August 1980

For this prize-winning mold, I used an Indian-head nickel! ↗

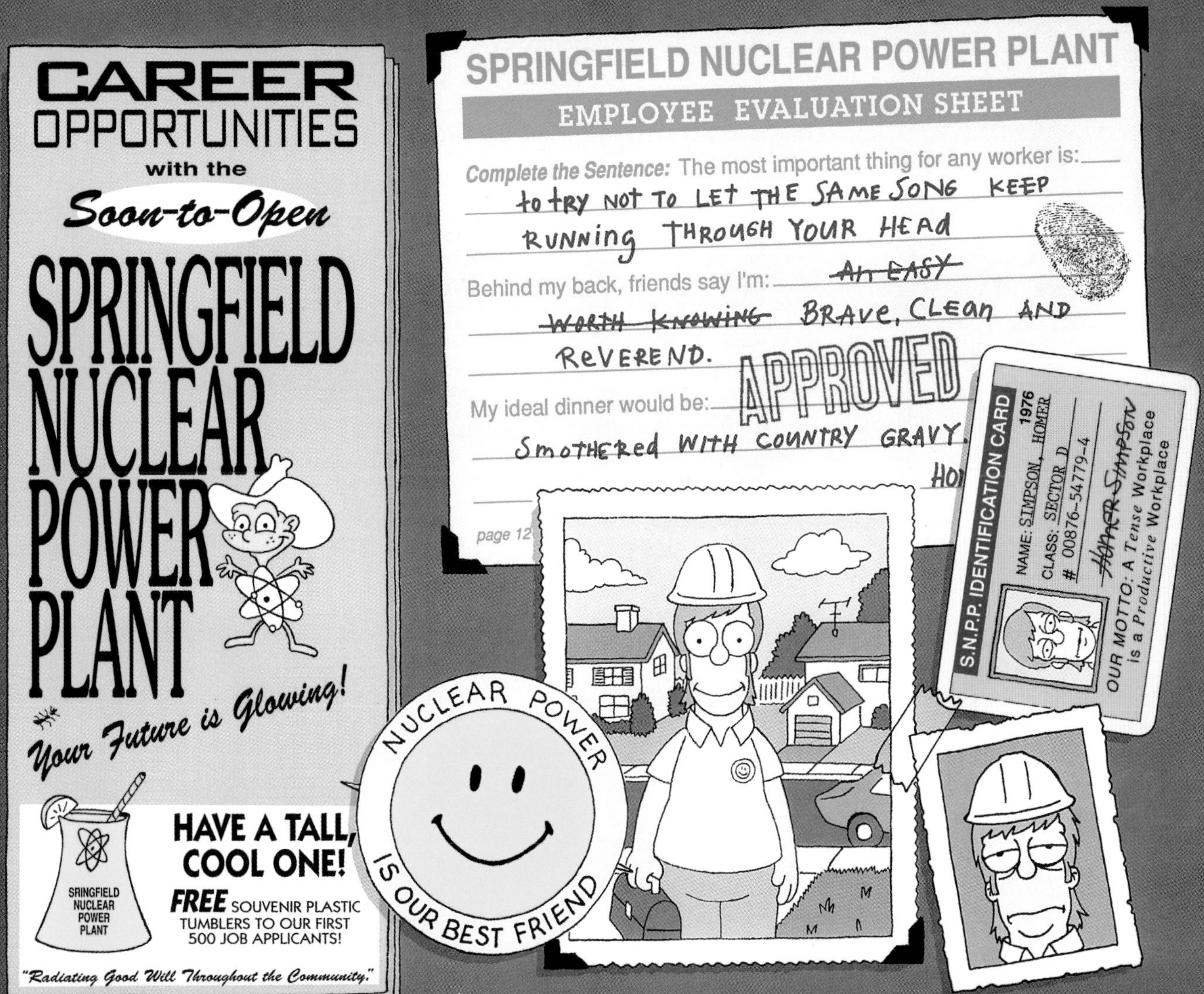
CAREER
OPPORTUNITIES
with the
Soon-to-Open
SPRINGFIELD
NUCLEAR
POWER
PLANT
Your Future is Glowing!
SRINGFIELD
NUCLEAR
POWER
PLANT
HAVE A TALL, COOL ONE!
FREE SOUVENIR PLASTIC TUMBLERS TO OUR FIRST 500 JOB APPLICANTS!
"Radiating Good Will Throughout the Community."
SPRINGFIELD NUCLEAR POWER PLANT
EMPLOYEE EVALUATION SHEET
Complete the Sentence: The most important thing for any worker is:
to try not to let the same song keep running through your head
Behind my back, friends say I'm: ~~An easy~~ ~~worth knowing~~ Brave, clean and reverend.
APPROVED
My ideal dinner would be:
Smothered with country gravy.
page 12
S.N.P.P. IDENTIFICATION CARD
1976
NAME: SIMPSON, HOMER
CLASS: SECTOR D
# 00876-54779-4
~~Homer Simpson~~
OUR MOTTO: A Tense Workplace is a Productive Workplace
NUCLEAR POWER IS OUR BEST FRIEND

Homer on the morning of his first day of work as a Power Plant employee!

...And at the end of his first day.

CERTIFICATE OF LIVE BIRTH
Child
Sex:
Time:
Place:
Parents
Doctor
Nurse
Barnacle Bill's
FREE!
Corncob Pipe
with purchase!
HOME PREGNANCY TEST
"Ahoy, Maties!
If the water turns blue, a baby for you!
If purple ye see, no baby thar be!
If ye test should fail, to a doctor set sail!"

My special little guy

# SPRINGFIELD GENERAL HOSPITAL

Founded 1925 — Established 1926

April 2

Dear Mr. and Mrs. Simpson,

After careful consideration and in view of complaints registered by other parents, we must ask that you remove your son from the hospital no later than 5 p.m. today, so that we may ensure the well-being of the other newborns.

As you usher baby Bert into the world, Dr. Mizzell, our director of maternity, has asked me to convey to you the following wish:

Don't bring him back.

Sincerely,

Hilda Beck

Hilda Beck, R.V.N.
Director of Nursing

*"Your illness is our business."*

5637 Underweather Blvd., Springfield — Right across from the Burns Memorial Golf Course.

CIGAR
EXPLO-DO
BE THE LIFE OF THE PARTY
THEY REALLY EXPLODE

It was awfully nice of them to keep Bart in a private room for the rest of the afternoon.

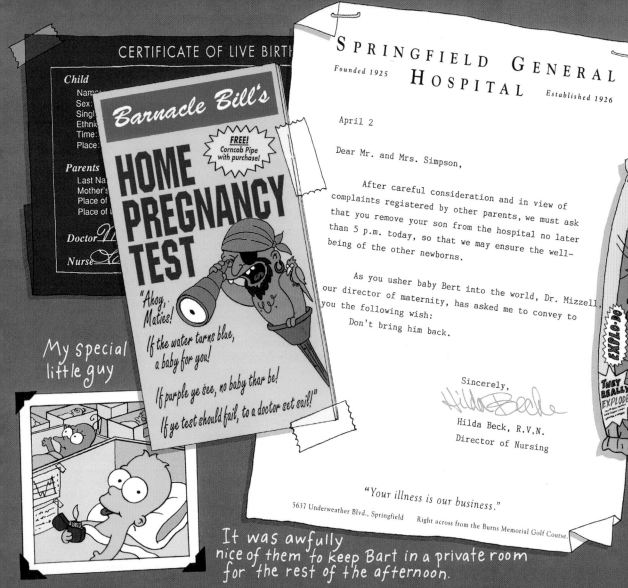

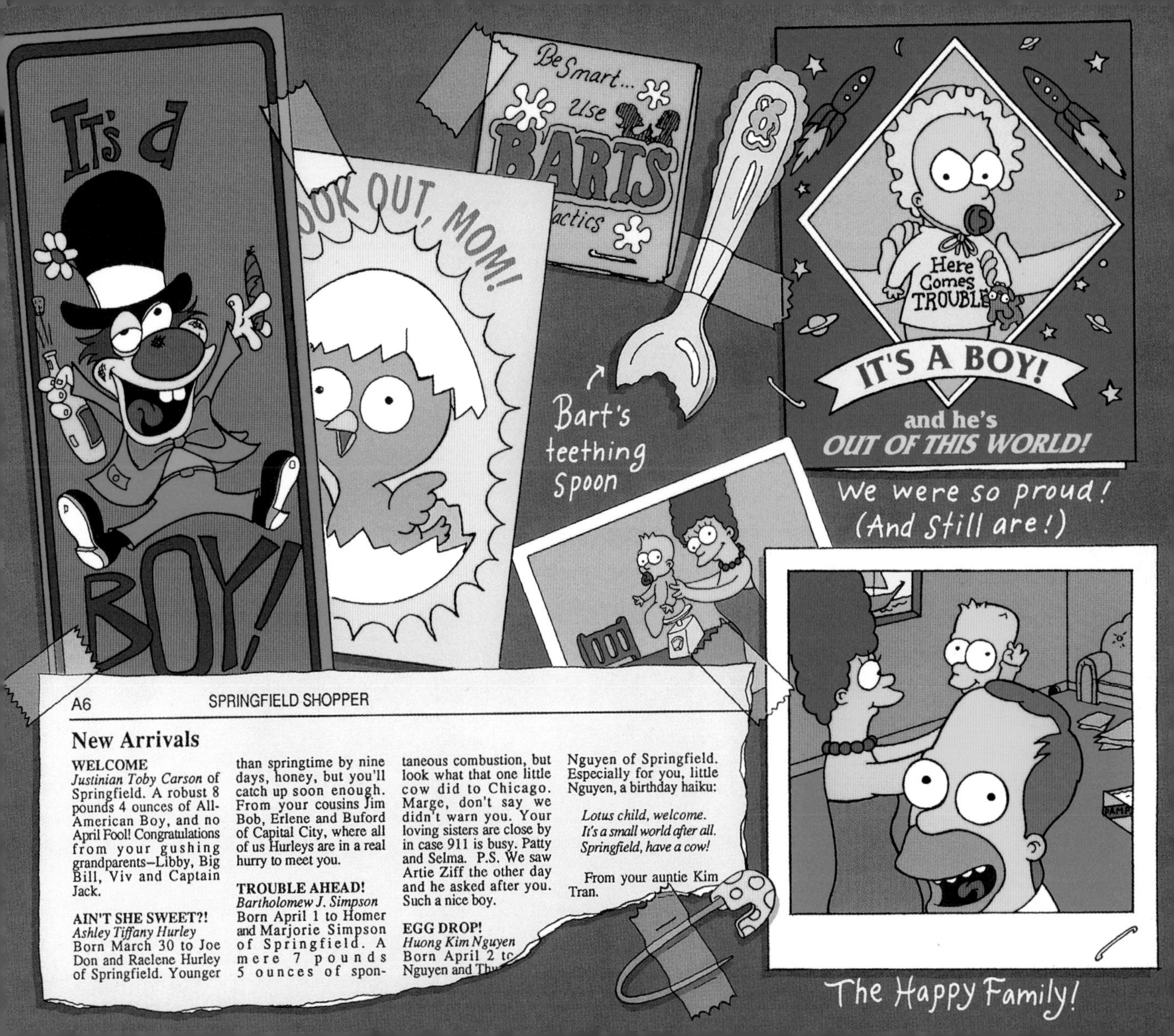

It's a
BOY!
OOK OUT, MOM!
Be Smart... Use BARTS
actics
Bart's teething Spoon
Here Comes TROUBLE
IT'S A BOY!
and he's OUT OF THIS WORLD!
We were so proud! (And Still are!)
A6 SPRINGFIELD SHOPPER
New Arrivals
WELCOME
Justinian Toby Carson of Springfield. A robust 8 pounds 4 ounces of All-American Boy, and no April Fool! Congratulations from your gushing grandparents–Libby, Big Bill, Viv and Captain Jack.
AIN'T SHE SWEET?!
Ashley Tiffany Hurley
Born March 30 to Joe Don and Raelene Hurley of Springfield. Younger than springtime by nine days, honey, but you'll catch up soon enough. From your cousins Jim Bob, Erlene and Buford of Capital City, where all of us Hurleys are in a real hurry to meet you.
TROUBLE AHEAD!
Bartholomew J. Simpson
Born April 1 to Homer and Marjorie Simpson of Springfield. A mere 7 pounds 5 ounces of spontaneous combustion, but look what that one little cow did to Chicago. Marge, don't say we didn't warn you. Your loving sisters are close by in case 911 is busy. Patty and Selma. P.S. We saw Artie Ziff the other day and he asked after you. Such a nice boy.
EGG DROP!
Huong Kim Nguyen
Born April 2 t
Nguyen and Th
Nguyen of Springfield. Especially for you, little Nguyen, a birthday haiku:
Lotus child, welcome.
It's a small world after all.
Springfield, have a cow!
From your auntie Kim Tran.
The Happy Family!

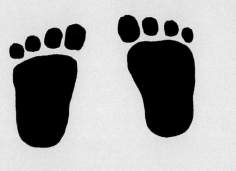

# SPRINGFIELD GENERAL HOSPITAL

Name: Simpson, Bartholomew

Parents: Marge/Homer

Date: April 1st

Weight: 7.2 lbs.

Length: 19.0"  Sex: ~~X~~ M

Delivering Physician:

*Dr. Julius Hibbert*

PATIENCE AND INSIGHT ARE NOT IN YOUR VOCABULARY — Homer's

YOU ARE ABOUT TO UNDERTAKE A LONG AND THANKLESS TASK ← Mine

*My first grey hair (and hopefully my last!)*

# SPRINGFIELD GENERAL HOSPITAL

**CLAIMS DEPT.**

We regret to inform you that unless the outstanding balance shown below is paid in full by September 15, we will have no alternative but to repossess your child.

*Delivery and Maternity Care*
Bartholomew J. Simpson
**Balance Due: $1,499.99**

**FINAL NOTICE**

B A R T H O L O M E W · J · S I M P

*I was so thrilled when the doctor announced:
"four toes on each foot, four fingers on each hand."*

# Bart and Lisa's first Haircuts.

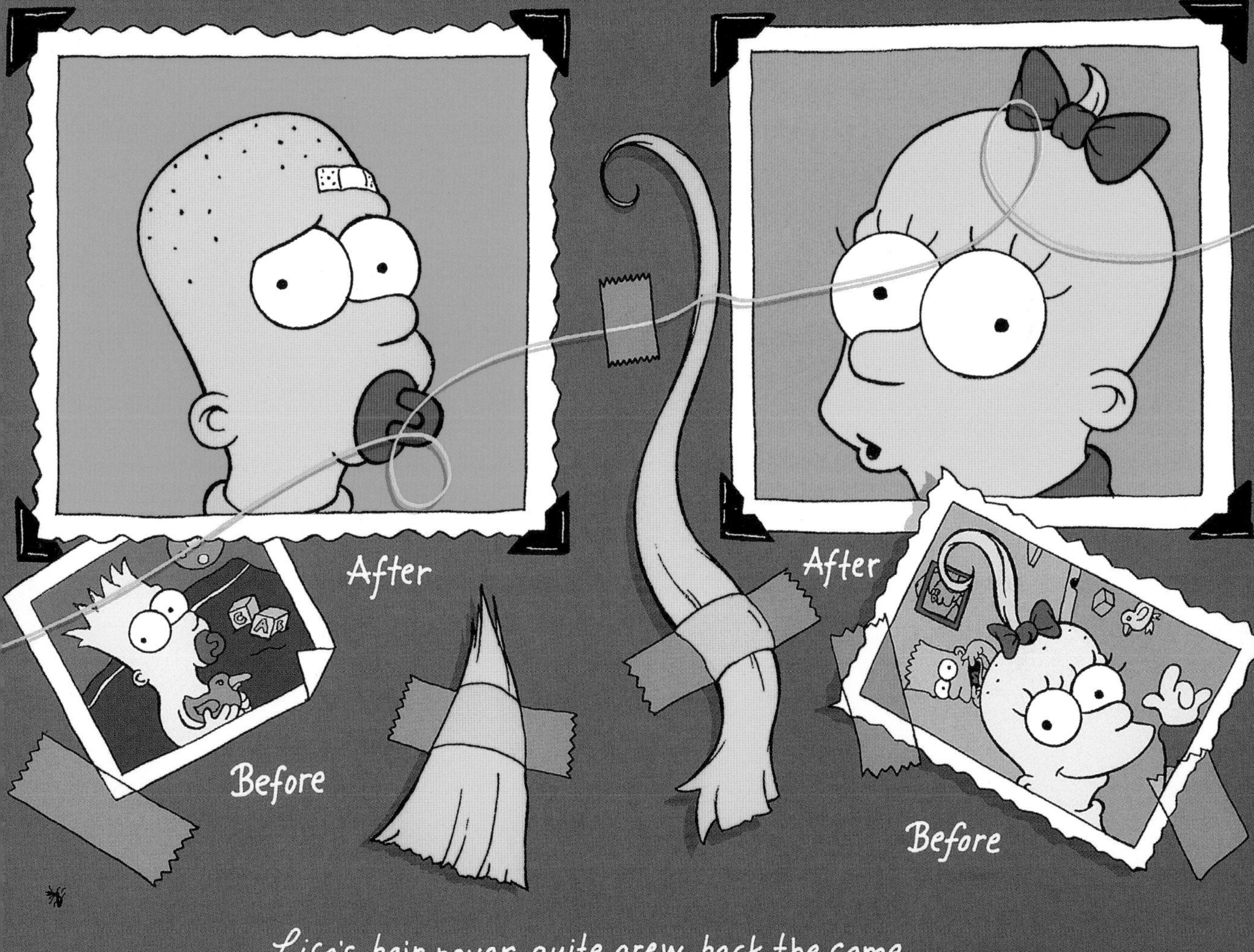
After
Before
After
Before

Lisa's hair never quite grew back the same.

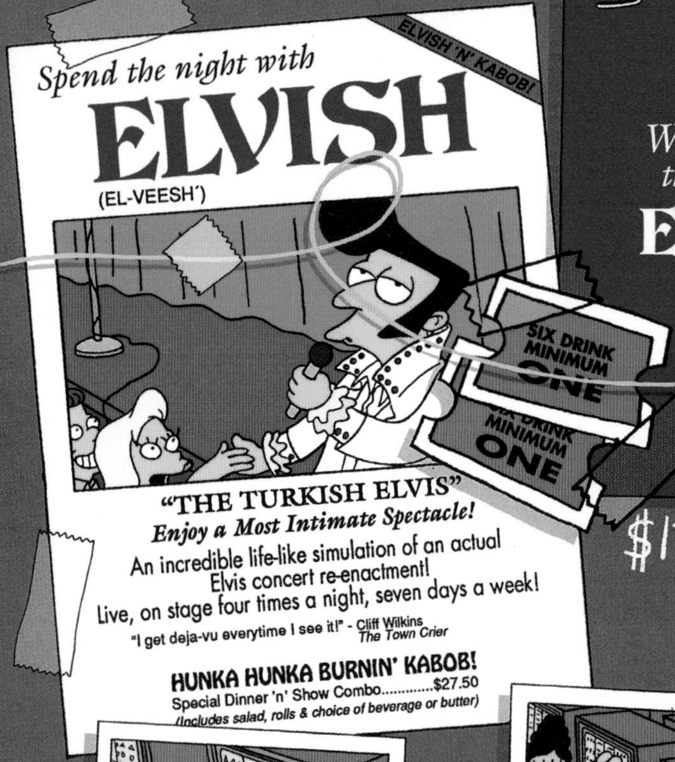
ELVISH 'N' KABOB!
Spend the night with
ELVISH
(EL-VEESH')
SIX DRINK MINIMUM
ONE
"THE TURKISH ELVIS"
Enjoy a Most Intimate Spectacle!
An incredible life-like simulation of an actual Elvis concert re-enactment!
Live, on stage four times a night, seven days a week!
"I get deja-vu everytime I see it!" - Cliff Wilkins The Town Crier
HUNKA HUNKA BURNIN' KABOB!
Special Dinner 'n' Show Combo.............$27.50
(Includes salad, rolls & choice of beverage or butter)

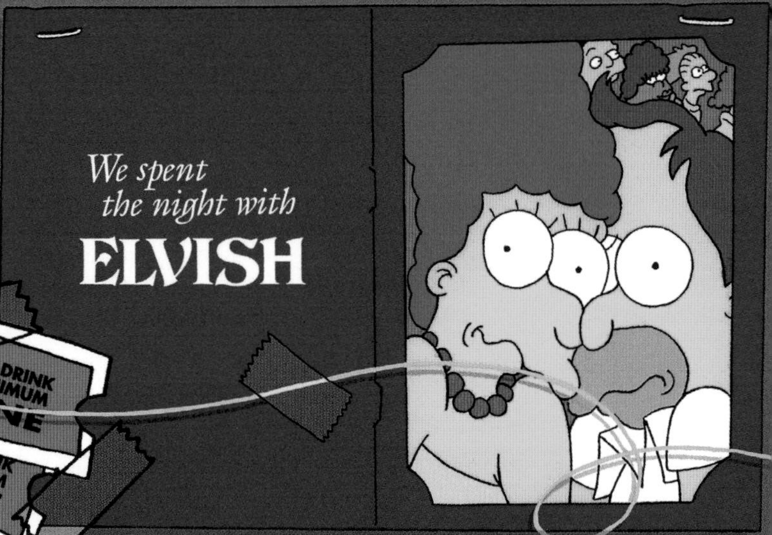
We spent
the night with
ELVISH

$17.95 for this STUPID PICTURE!
THEY GET YOU DRUNK THEN THEY TAKE YOUR MONEY!

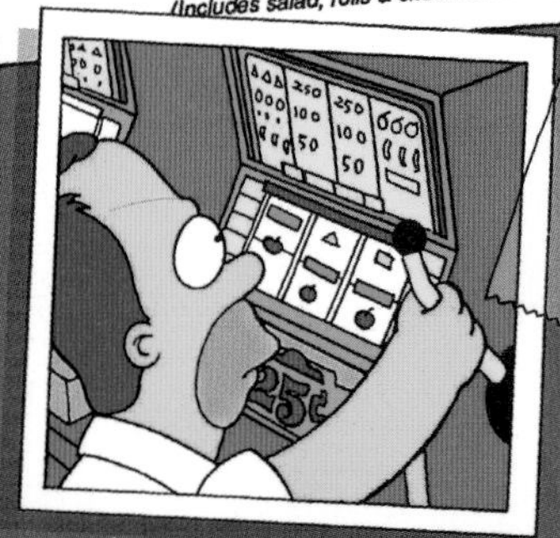

Homer at the slots.
He kept saying he "felt lucky", so I couldn't stop him.

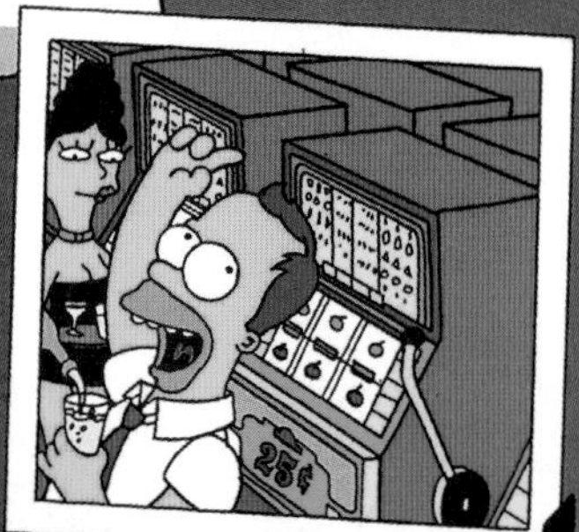

Jackpot!

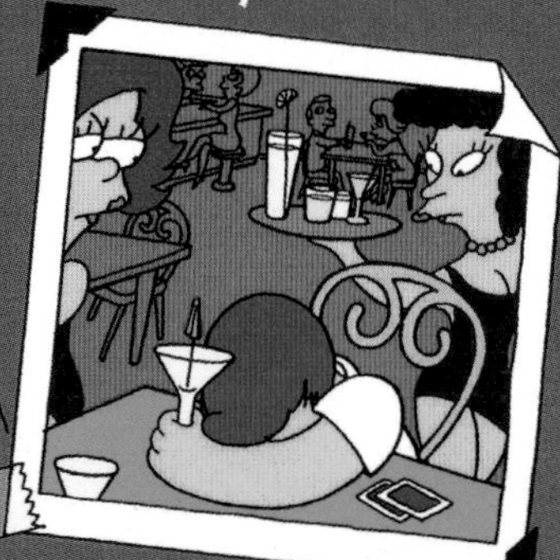

Homer after he lost the entire $11,158.97

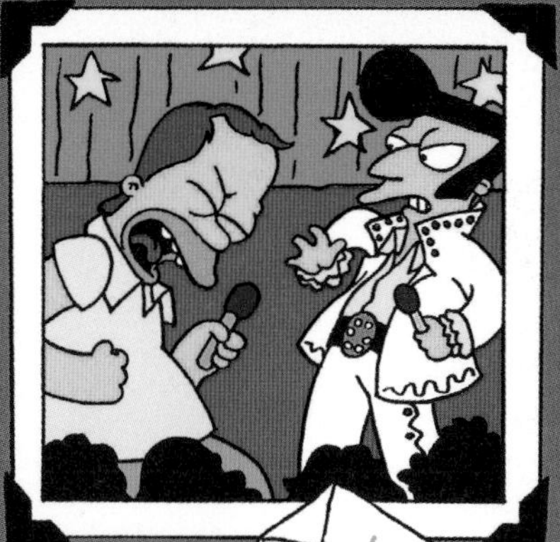

Homer's Shining Hour

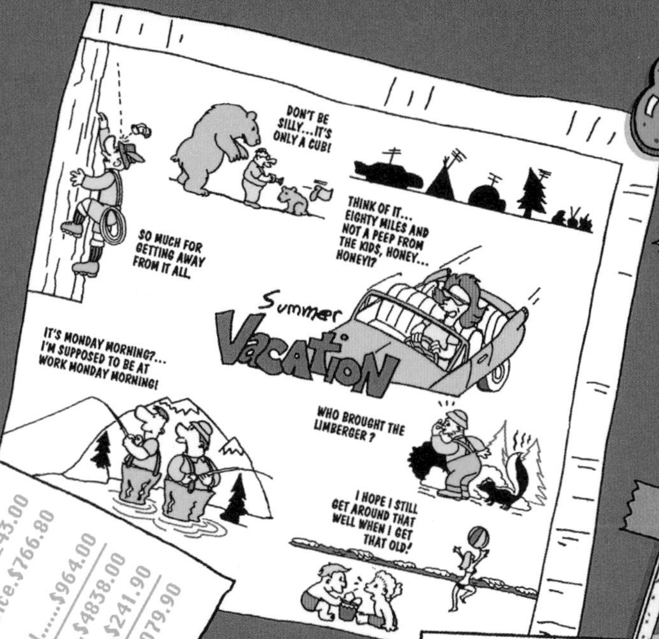
DON'T BE SILLY...IT'S ONLY A CUB!
THINK OF IT... EIGHTY MILES AND NOT A PEEP FROM THE KIDS, HONEY... HONEY!?
SO MUCH FOR GETTING AWAY FROM IT ALL.
Summer Vacation
IT'S MONDAY MORNING?... I'M SUPPOSED TO BE AT WORK MONDAY MORNING!
WHO BROUGHT THE LIMBERGER ?
I HOPE I STILL GET AROUND THAT WELL WHEN I GET THAT OLD!

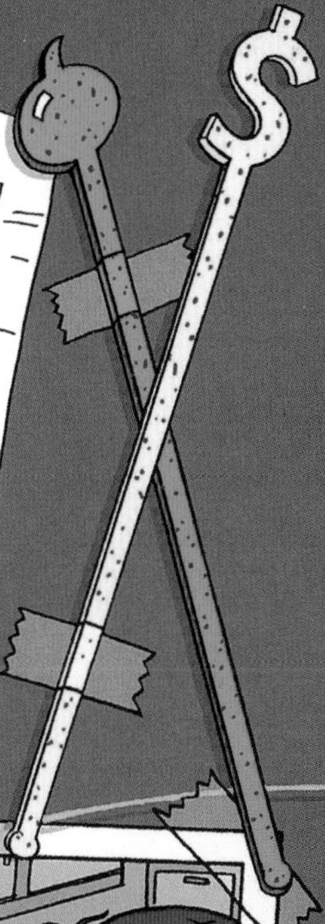

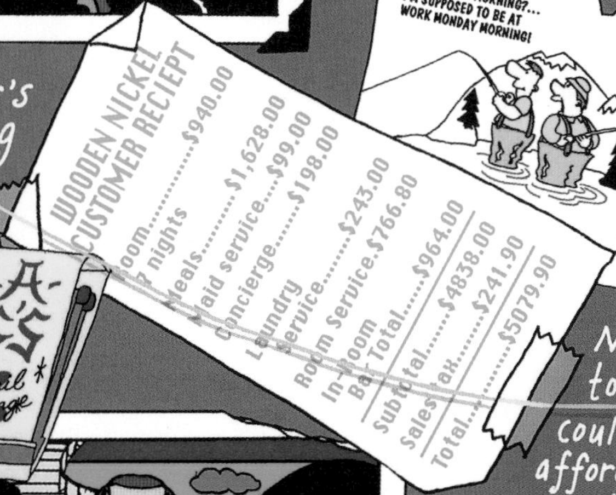

WOODEN NICKEL
CUSTOMER RECIEPT

| | |
|---|---|
| Room 7 nights | $940.00 |
| Meals | $1,628.00 |
| Maid service | $99.00 |
| Concierge | $198.00 |
| Laundry Service | $243.00 |
| Room Service | $766.80 |
| In-Room Bar Total | $964.00 |
| Subtotal | $4838.00 |
| Sales tax | $241.90 |
| Total | $5079.90 |

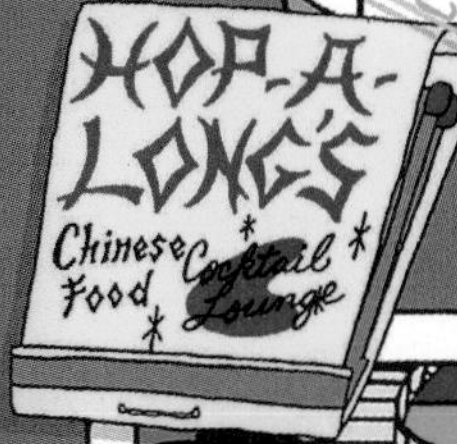
HOP-A-LONG'S
Chinese Food
Cocktail Lounge

Needless to say, we could not afford to pay our bill.

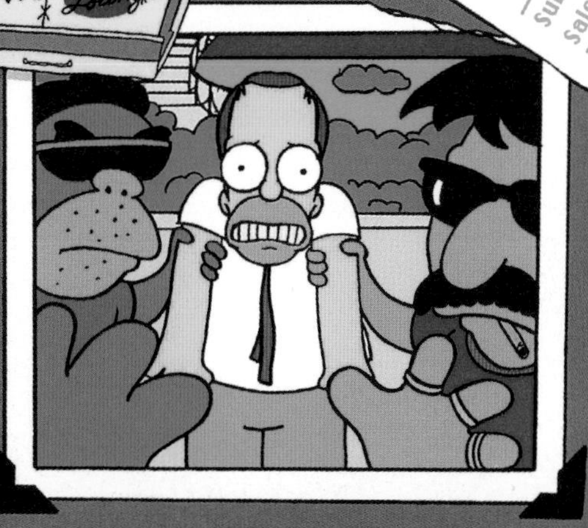

These nice men wanted to take Homer for a ride, but I assured them it wasn't necessary.

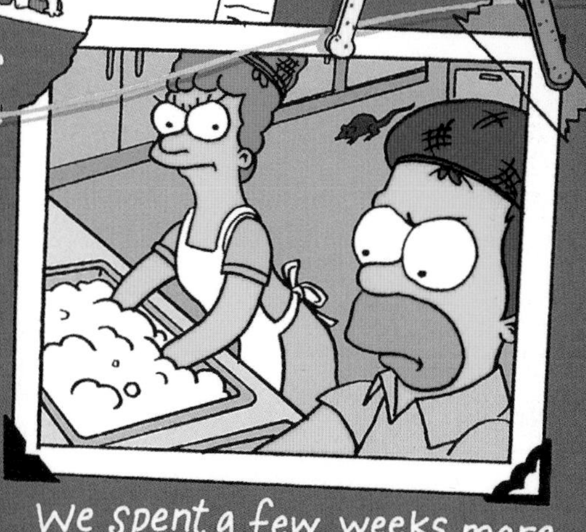

We spent a few weeks more at the old Wooden Nickel than we'd planned.

*Greetings from* **POTATO ROCK**

**NATIONAL PARK**

A visit to our state's most wondrous rock formation

Homer doing "the Hustle" atop P.R.

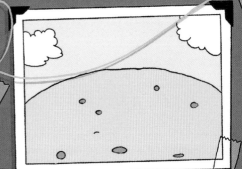

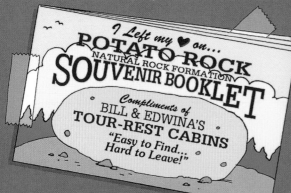

I Left my ♥ on...
**POTATO ROCK**
NATURAL ROCK FORMATION
**SOUVENIR BOOKLET**

*Compliments of*
BILL & EDWINA'S
**TOUR-REST CABINS**
"Easy to Find...
Hard to Leave!"

He joked, "Where's the sour cream and chives?" just before he fell off.

Homer was determined not to let this happen again. He bought a new "Liquid Center" ball in the pro shop right afterwards and couldn't wait to try it...

PARTYING DOWN!

Apu donated 76 lbs. of beef jerky to the cause!

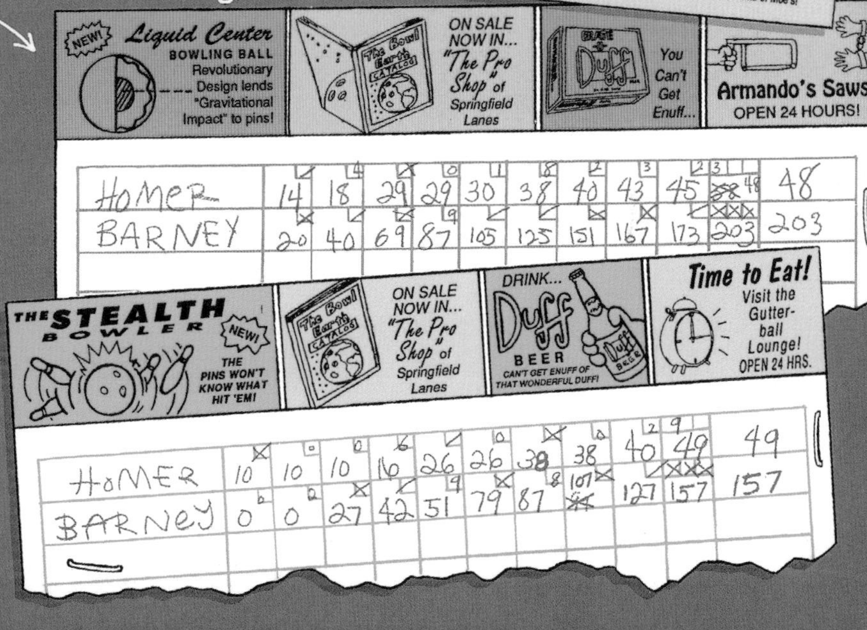

**NEW! Liquid Center BOWLING BALL** Revolutionary Design lends "Gravitational Impact" to pins!

ON SALE NOW IN... "The Pro Shop" of Springfield Lanes

You Can't Get Enuff!

**Armando's Saws** OPEN 24 HOURS!

| | 1 | 2 | 3 | 4 | 5 | 6 | 7 | 8 | 9 | 10 | |
|---|---|---|---|---|---|---|---|---|---|---|---|
| HOMER | 14 | 18 | 29 | 29 | 30 | 38 | 40 | 43 | 45 | 48 | 48 |
| BARNEY | 20 | 40 | 69 | 87 | 105 | 125 | 151 | 167 | 173 | 203 | 203 |

Homer in Rare Form

# THE STEALTH BOWLER

**NEW!** THE PINS WON'T KNOW WHAT HIT 'EM!

ON SALE NOW IN... "The Pro Shop" of Springfield Lanes

**DRINK... Duff BEER** CAN'T GET ENUFF OF THAT WONDERFUL DUFF!

**Time to Eat!** Visit the Gutter-ball Lounge! OPEN 24 HRS.

| | 1 | 2 | 3 | 4 | 5 | 6 | 7 | 8 | 9 | 10 | |
|---|---|---|---|---|---|---|---|---|---|---|---|
| HOMER | 10 | 10 | 10 | 16 | 26 | 26 | 38 | 38 | 40 | 49 | 49 |
| BARNEY | 0 | 0 | 27 | 42 | 51 | 79 | 87 | 107 | 127 | 157 | 157 |

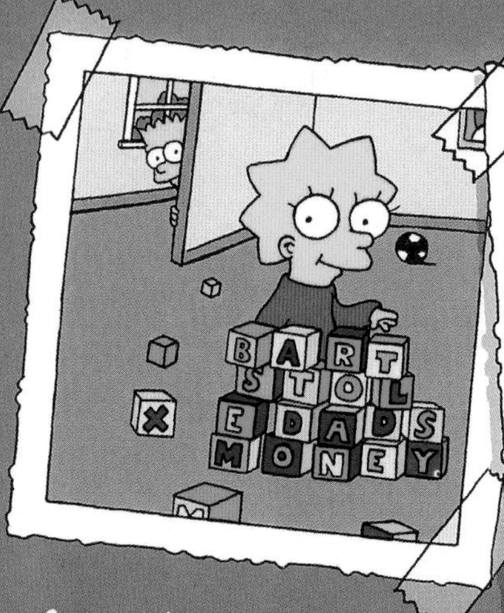
BART
STOL
E DADS
MONEY

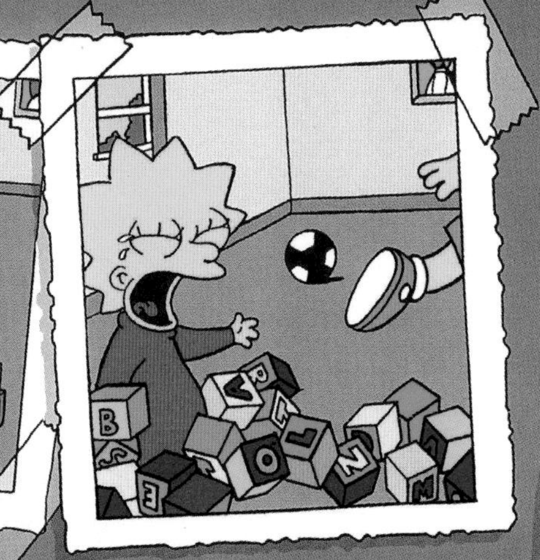

Lisa at 22 months.
Such a perceptive child!

Yet quite sensitive.

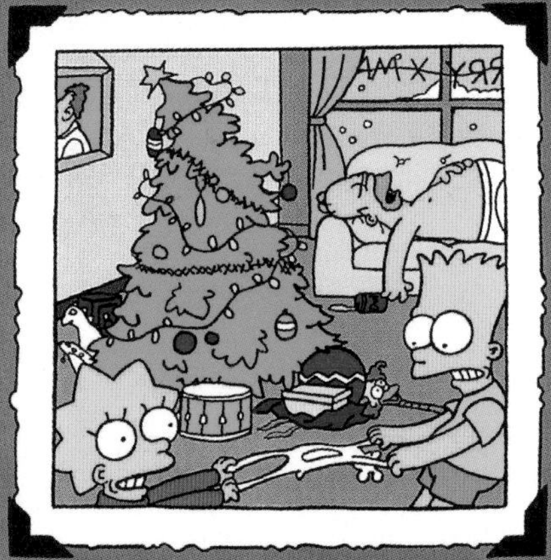

Family Xmas

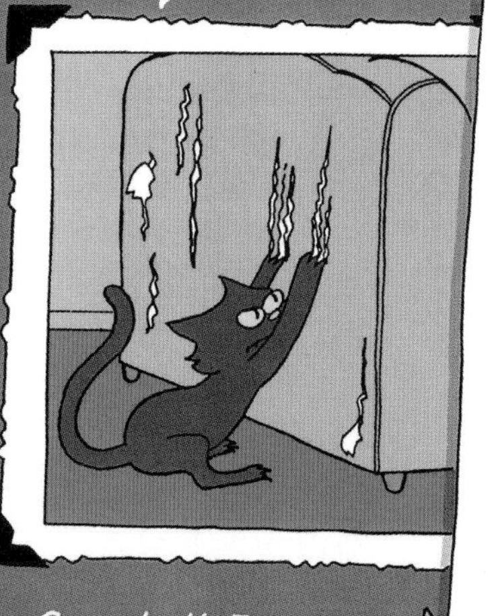

Snowball I as a kitten. She was cute, but she was BAD!

THE FASTEST FOOD ALIVE!

# KRUSTY BURGER

MENU

*Indescribable*
**KRUSTER-ITOS**..............$1.29

*South-of-the-Border-Style*
**DOGMALES**.....................$1.32

*100% Recycled*
**CHEEZE-RINGS**................ 79¢

*Double-Dipped, Fat-Fried*
**KORN-KATS**...................... 99¢

*The Original All Meat By-Products*
**KRUSTY BURGER**...........$1.29
*with cheese*..............................add 50¢
*with bun*....................................add 75¢
*with napkin*...............................add 15¢

*Fried-for-Hours*
**POTATO EYES**................$1.15

*Lo-Cal Diet Special*
**SALAD-ON-A-STIK**.........$1.29

*Cotton Candy & Hot Dog Delite*
**WEENIE-ON-A-CLOUD**..... 99¢

*Eat 'Em & Weep*
**ONION LOGS**.................... 79¢

Springfield kindergarten

**REPORT CARD**

Name: SIMPSON, LISA

Teacher: MRS. WELLSLEY

| | |
|---|---|
| Alphabet | A |
| Storytime | A |
| Cookies & Milk Time | A |
| Recess | B |
| Songtime | A |
| Numbers | A |
| | A |

Mrs. Simpson,

Lisa is a bright and introspective child. The word "gifted" may be applicable. Although perhaps she is too introspective and gifted for her own good.

Mrs. Wellsley

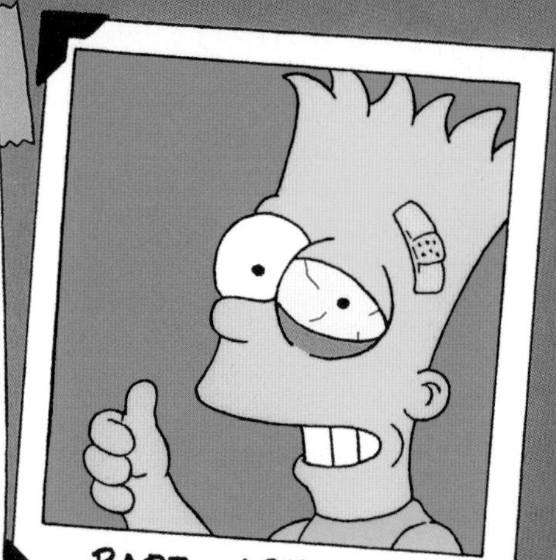

BART - AGE 8

Bart's first black eye. (and not his last, I'm afraid.)

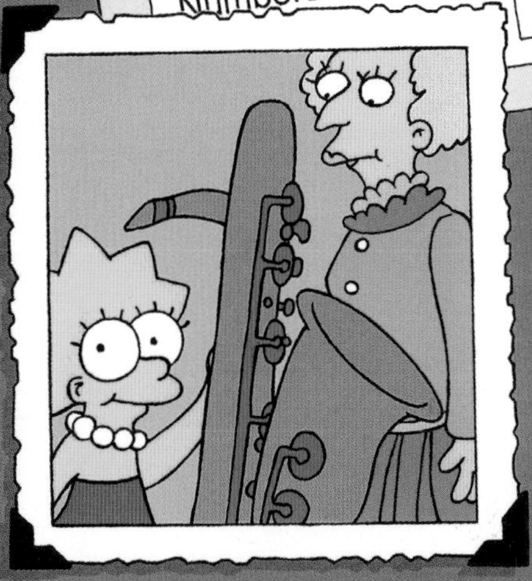

Lisa with her kindergarten teacher, Mrs. Wellseley. (And her baritone Sax) Age 5.

I had a cat named
Snowball--
She died! She died!
Mom said she was
sleeping--
She lied! She lied!
Why oh why is my
cat dead?
Couldn't that Chrysler
hit me instead?
- Lisa Simpson

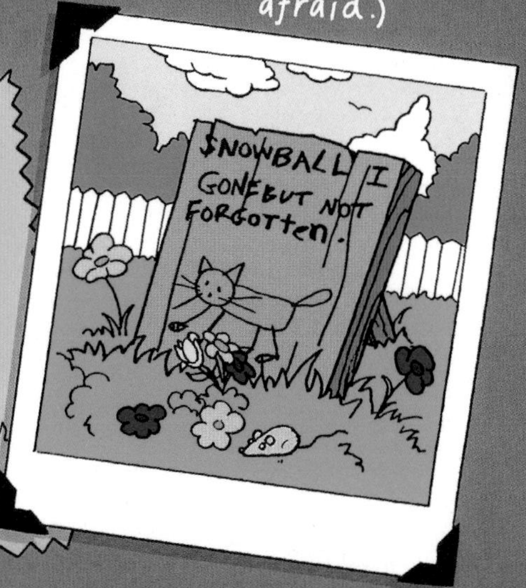
SNOWBALL I
GONE BUT NOT
FORGOTTEN.

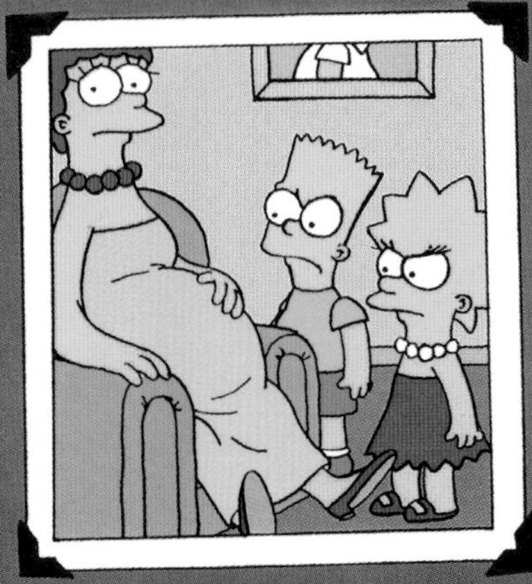

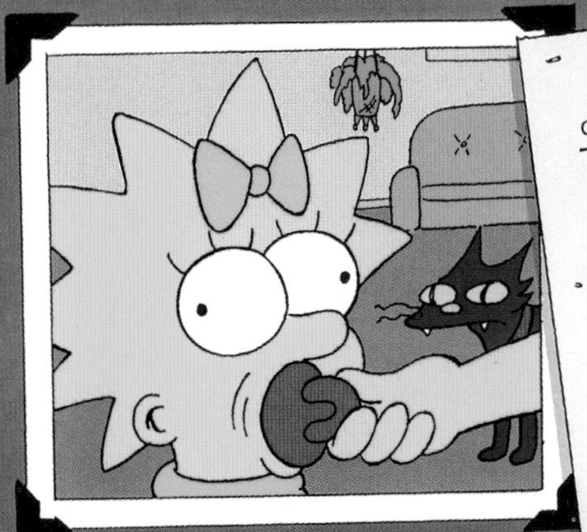

Here I am pregnant with Little Maggie!

Maggie was such an easy child! By the time she came along, I knew all the tricks!

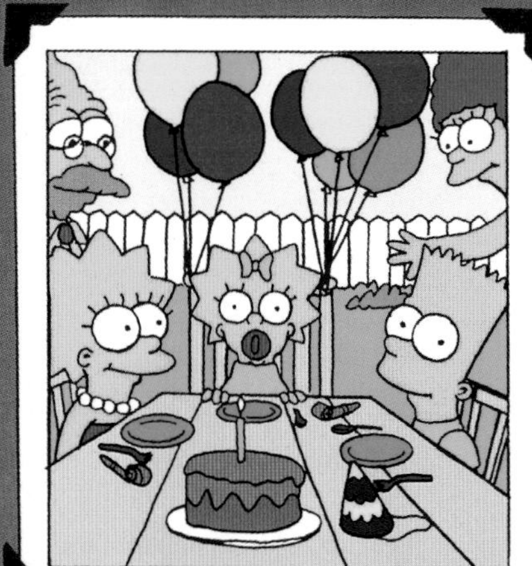

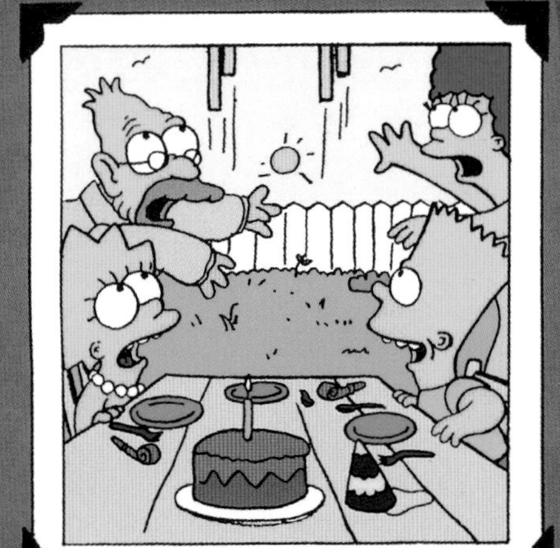

Maggie's First Birthday

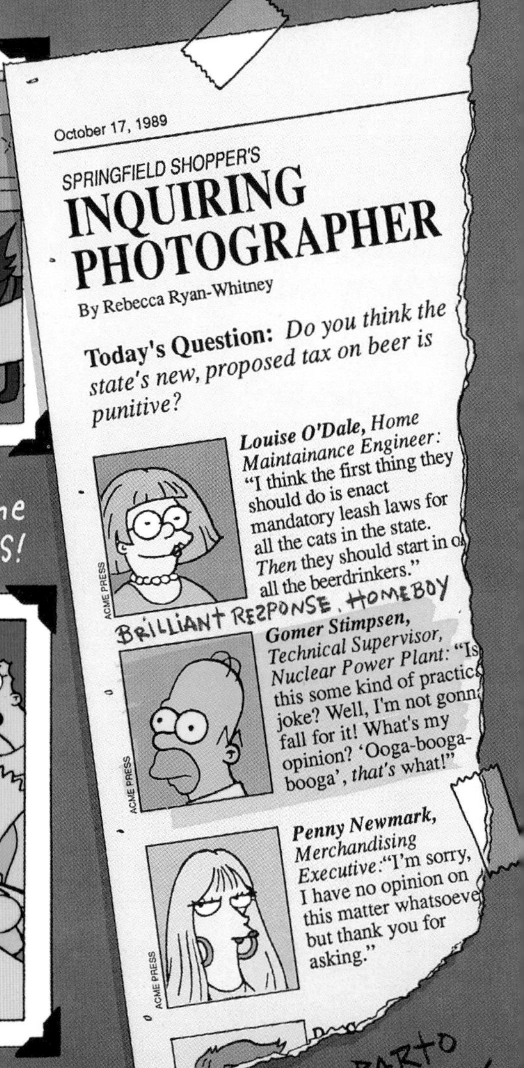

October 17, 1989

SPRINGFIELD SHOPPER'S

# INQUIRING PHOTOGRAPHER

By Rebecca Ryan-Whitney

**Today's Question:** *Do you think the state's new, proposed tax on beer is punitive?*

ACME PRESS

***Louise O'Dale,** Home Maintainance Engineer:* "I think the first thing they should do is enact mandatory leash laws for all the cats in the state. *Then* they should start in o all the beerdrinkers."

BRILLIANT RESPONSE, HOMEBOY

ACME PRESS

***Gomer Stimpsen,** Technical Supervisor, Nuclear Power Plant:* "Is this some kind of practic joke? Well, I'm not gonn fall for it! What's my opinion? 'Ooga-booga-booga', *that's* what!"

ACME PRESS

***Penny Newmark,** Merchandising Executive:* "I'm sorry, I have no opinion on this matter whatsoeve but thank you for asking."

EL BARTO WAS HERE

I was So, so, so proud! ↓

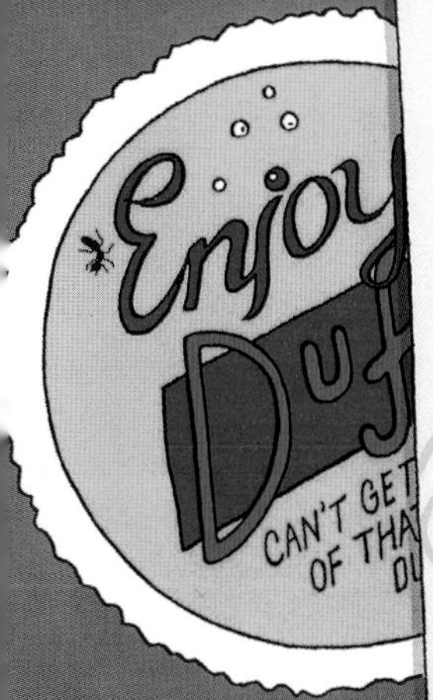

Enjoy
CAN'T GET
OF THAT


November 4, 1989

## Murphy's Tenor Evokes Youthful Anxiety

By Jiff Johnson, *Shopper Music Critic*

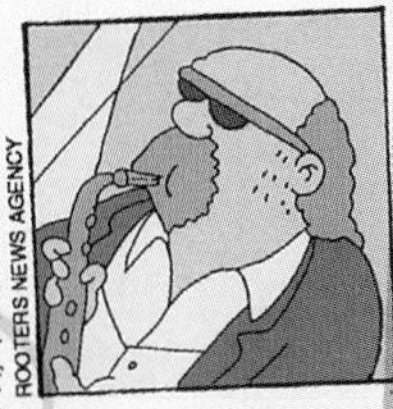
ROOTERS NEWS AGENCY

Bleeding Gums Murphy knows suffering so well you might mistake him for suffering's twin brother.

Last night at the Jazz Hole, however, Springfield's resident jazzman extraodinaire bent the reed of his tenor sax in the direction of second grader Lisa Simpson.

Murphy introduced the 7-year-old Miss Simpson's composition "The Manipulative Daddy Blues" to an appreciative Hole audience.

What makes this collaboration work is the juxtaposition of Murphy's well-worn (but never tired) voice of experience with the stark, honest perception of Simpson's youthful dilemma: the need to function in an oppressive home environment while simultaneously yearning for a liberated artisti space.

Murphy's quarte appearing indefinitely a Springfield's leading jaz venue, continues to brea new ground in this mo American of all music idioms.

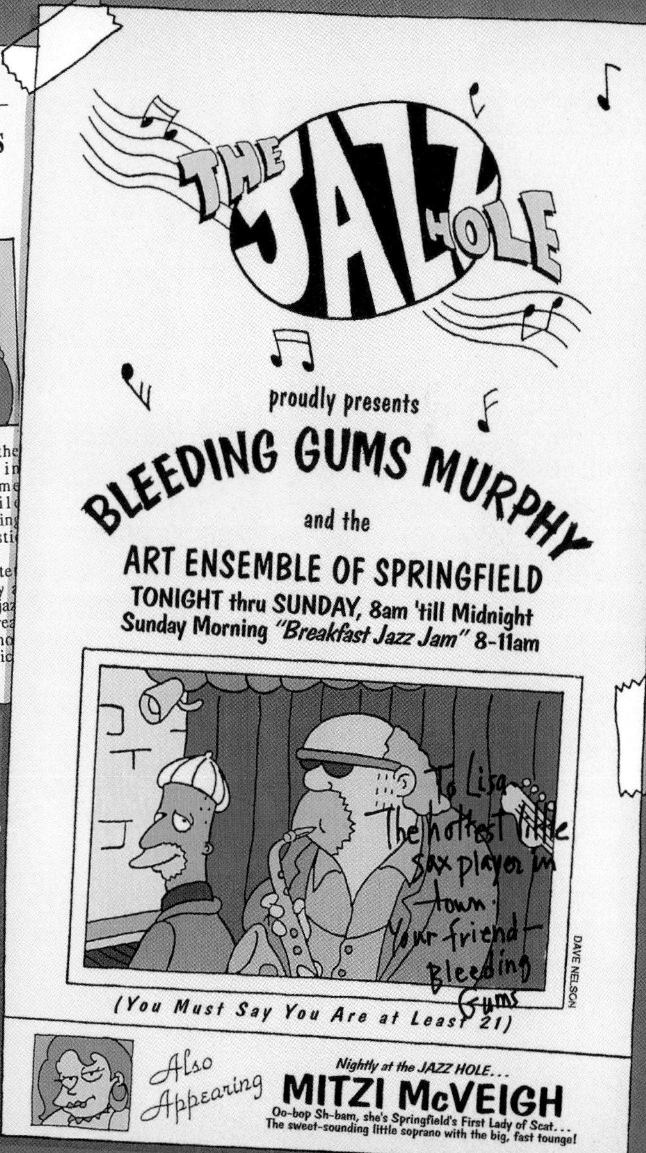

THE JAZZ HOLE
proudly presents
BLEEDING GUMS MURPHY
and the
ART ENSEMBLE OF SPRINGFIELD
TONIGHT thru SUNDAY, 8am 'till Midnight
Sunday Morning "Breakfast Jazz Jam" 8-11am
To Lisa— The hottest little sax player in town. Your friend— Bleeding Gums
DAVE NELSON
(You Must Say You Are at Least 21)
Also Appearing
Nightly at the JAZZ HOLE...
MITZI McVEIGH
Oo-bop Sh-bam, she's Springfield's First Lady of Scat...
The sweet-sounding little soprano with the big, fast tounge!


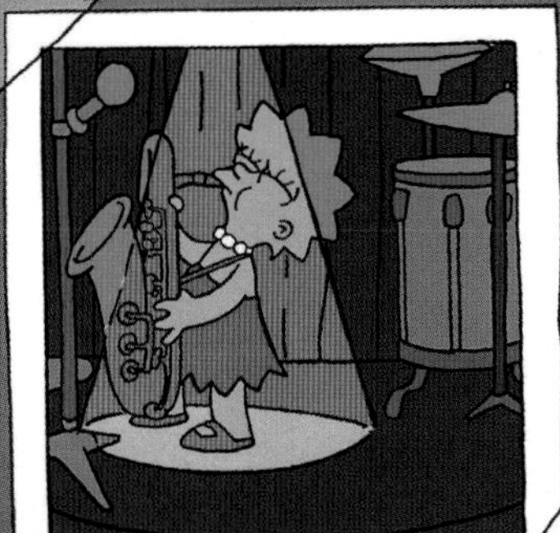

I don't know much about this man's music, but I do wish he'd do something about that name!

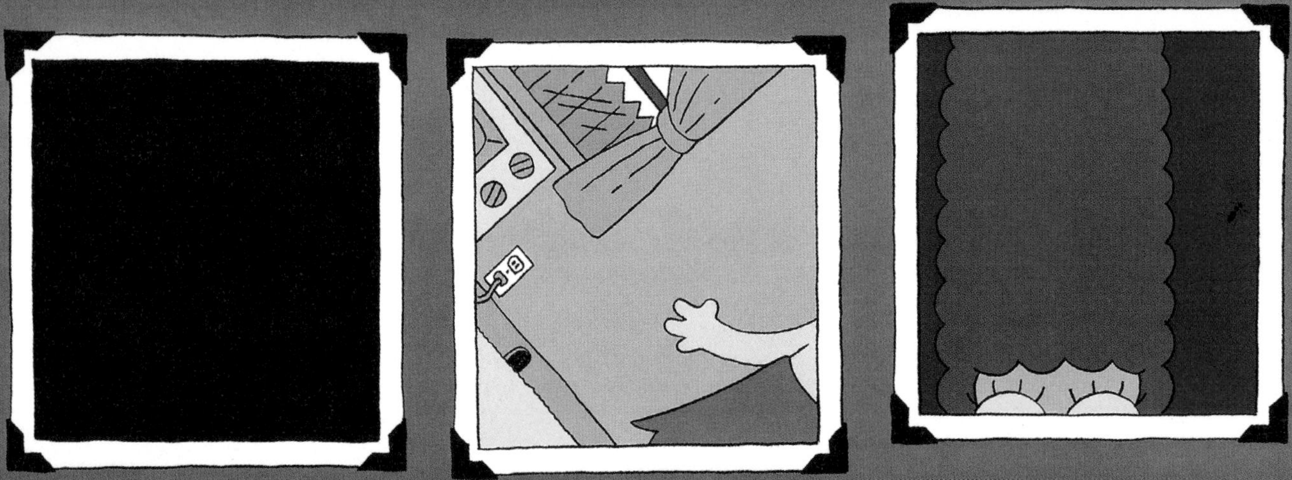

The Day Homer Got His New Camera

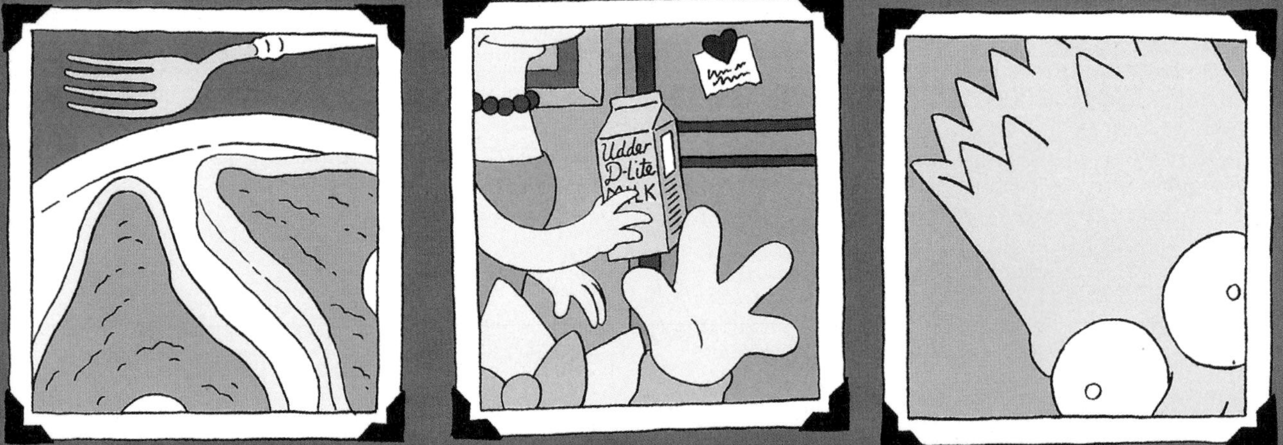
Udder
D-Lite

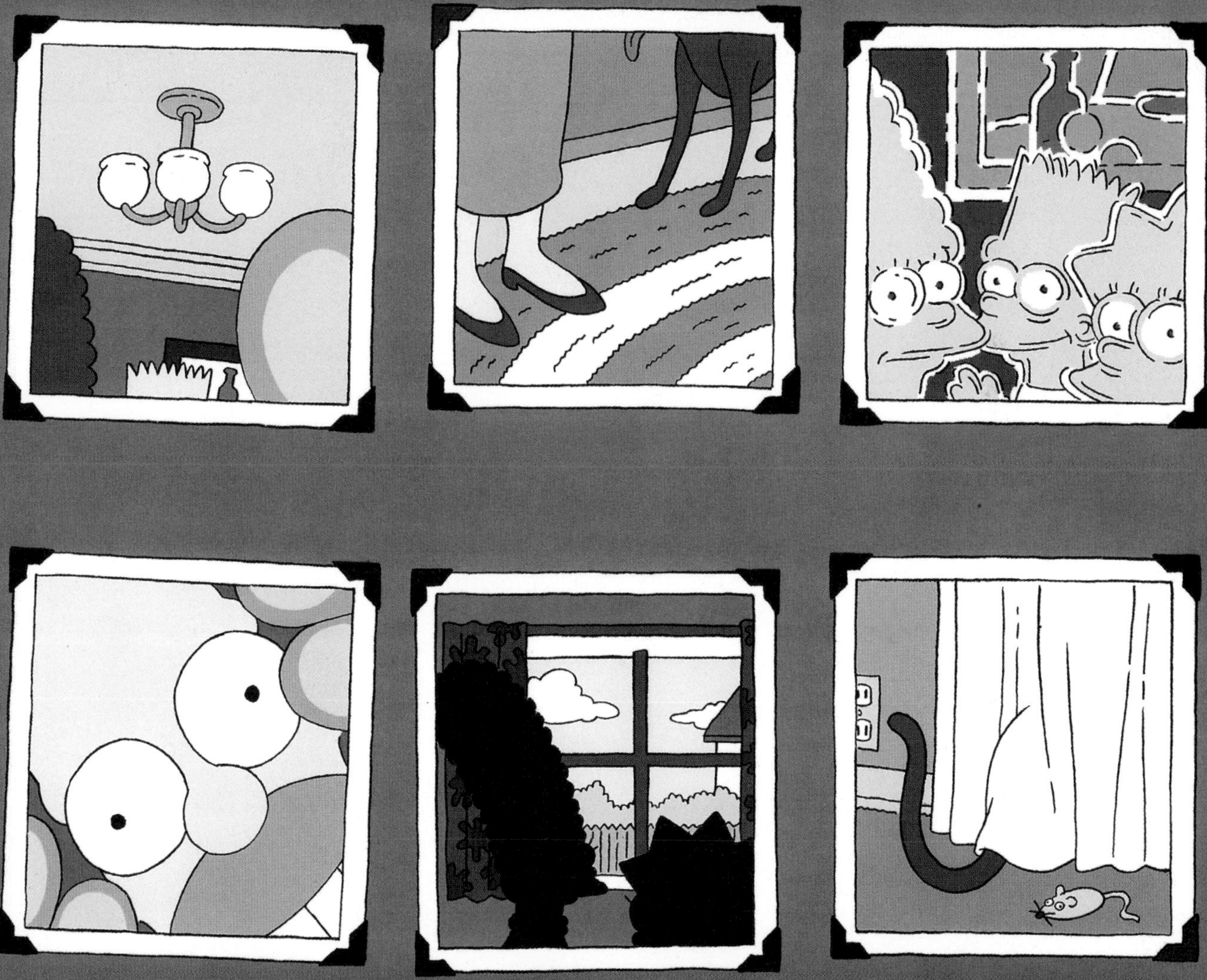

Poem #254

"Optimism" is the thing with fur
That curls upon the sofa
And dreams of Happy Little Elves
And never snores -- at all

And in the grimmest hour
    is there --
and annoying though my family be
They cannot bestir the Gentle Beast
That keeps my spirit free.

So long I've nurtured it
And thus I'll be repaid.
For it shall, I know it shall
Bring a pony unto me.

Lisa Simpson (age 7)

I didn't even know she had a pet named "Optimism"! I just hope it's not some sort of rodent.

Maggie's First Step (well, actually seconds after her first step)

Maggie's second step

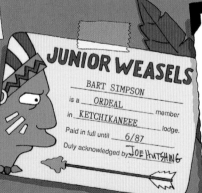

JUNIOR WEASELS

BART SIMPSON

is a __ORDEAL__ member
in __KETCHIKANEEE__ lodge.

Paid in full until __6/87__

Duly acknowledged by __JOE HUTSHING__

Bart's arrowhead, which he found at Camp Itchawanda while hunting for "snipes."

Luckily, Bart was a lousy shot.

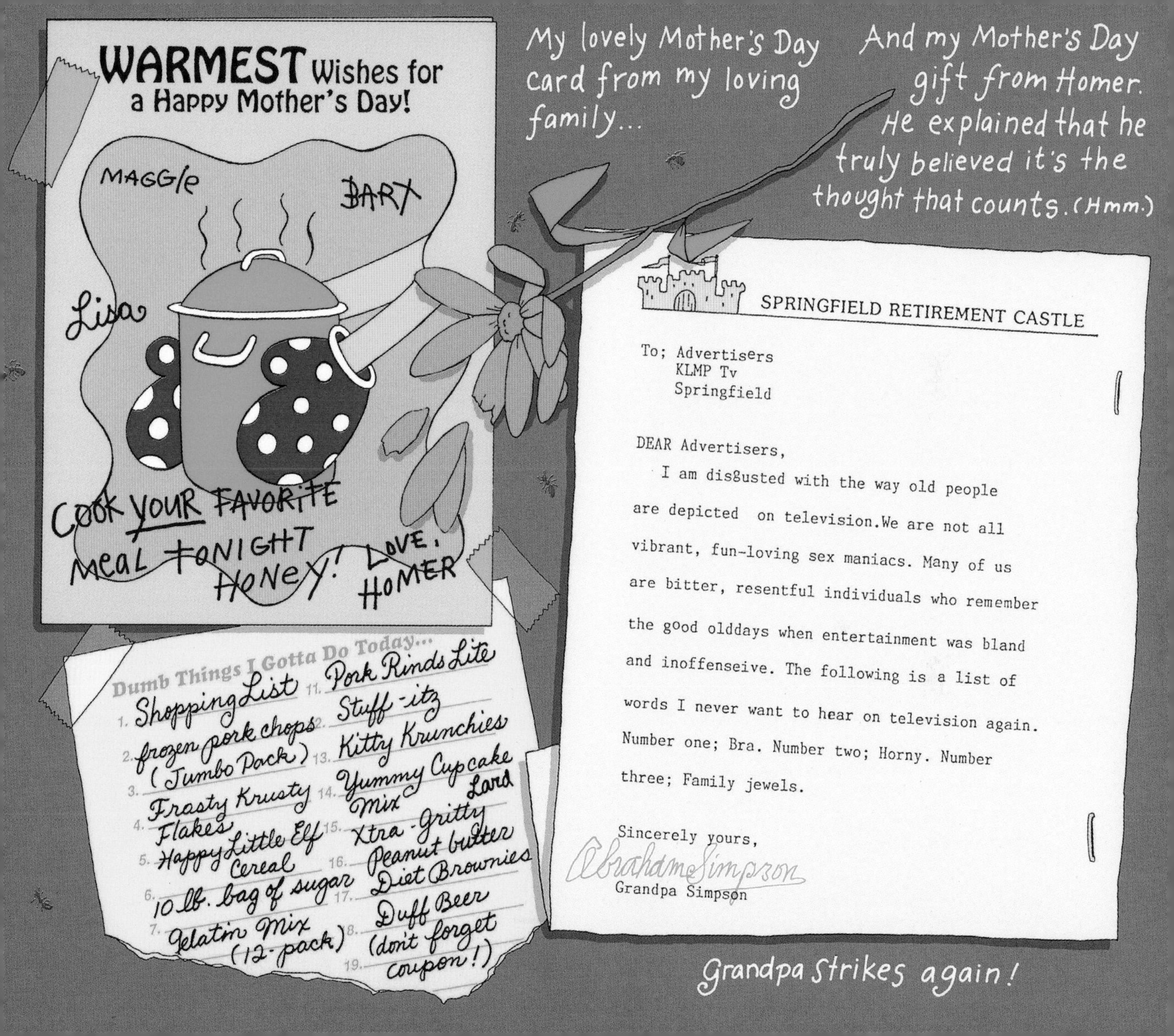
WARMEST Wishes for a Happy Mother's Day!
MAGGIE
BART
Lisa
COOK YOUR FAVORITE MEAL TONIGHT HONEY! LOVE, HOMER
My lovely Mother's Day card from my loving family...
And my Mother's Day gift from Homer. He explained that he truly believed it's the thought that counts. (Hmm.)
SPRINGFIELD RETIREMENT CASTLE
To; Advertisers
KLMP Tv
Springfield
DEAR Advertisers,
I am disgusted with the way old people are depicted on television.We are not all vibrant, fun-loving sex maniacs. Many of us are bitter, resentful individuals who remember the good olddays when entertainment was bland and inoffenseive. The following is a list of words I never want to hear on television again. Number one; Bra. Number two; Horny. Number three; Family jewels.
Sincerely yours,
Abraham Simpson
Grandpa Simpson
Dumb Things I Gotta Do Today...
1. Shopping List
2. frozen pork chops (Jumbo Pack)
3. Frasty Krusty
4. Flakes
5. Happy Little Elf Cereal
6. 10 lb. bag of sugar
7. Gelatin Mix (12-pack)
8.
11. Pork Rinds Lite
12. Stuff-itz
13. Kitty Krunchies
14. Yummy Cupcake Mix
15. Xtra-Gritty Lard
16. Peanut butter
17. Diet Brownies
18. Duff Beer (don't forget coupon!)
19.
Grandpa strikes again!

Memories of a vacation Homer would like to forget

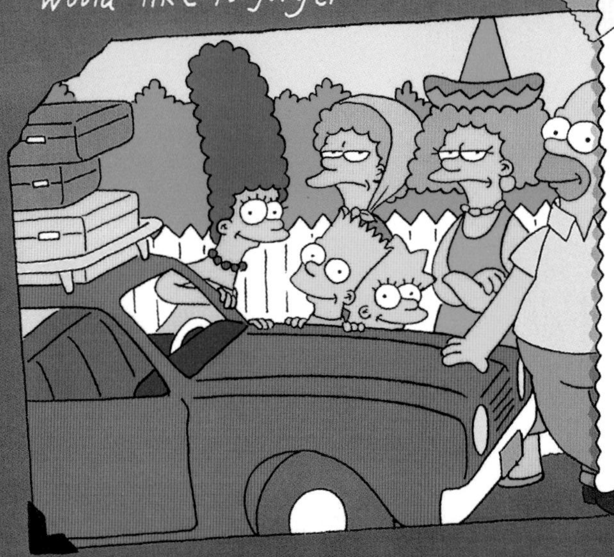

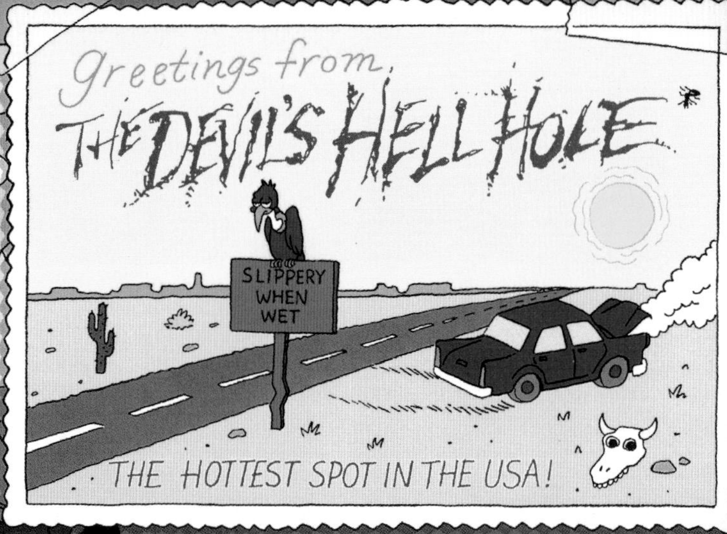
greetings from,
THE DEVIL'S HELL HOLE
SLIPPERY WHEN WET
THE HOTTEST SPOT IN THE USA!

Patty and Selma said the resorts of the Devil's Hell-Hole region are the playgrounds of the rich and famous. But I can't imagine rich people wanting to be so darned uncomfortably hot and sweaty!

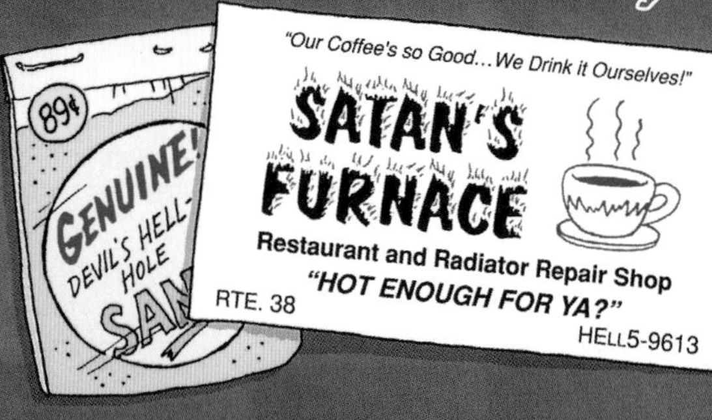
89¢
GENUINE!
DEVIL'S HELL-HOLE
"Our Coffee's so Good... We Drink it Ourselves!"
SATAN'S FURNACE
Restaurant and Radiator Repair Shop
"HOT ENOUGH FOR YA?"
RTE. 38
HELL5-9613

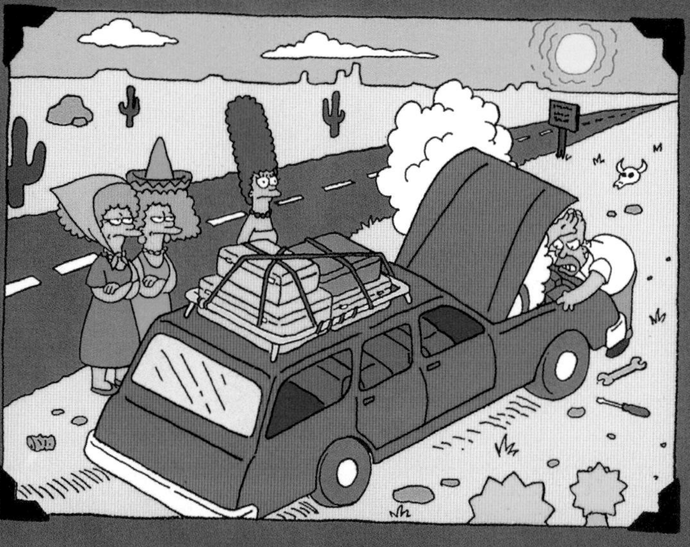

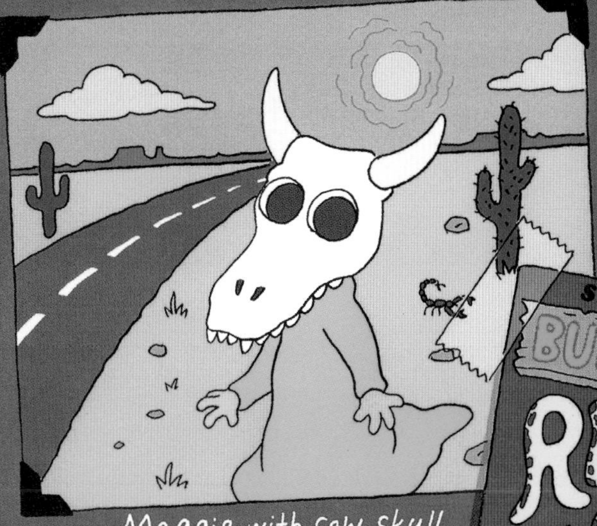

Maggie with cow skull.

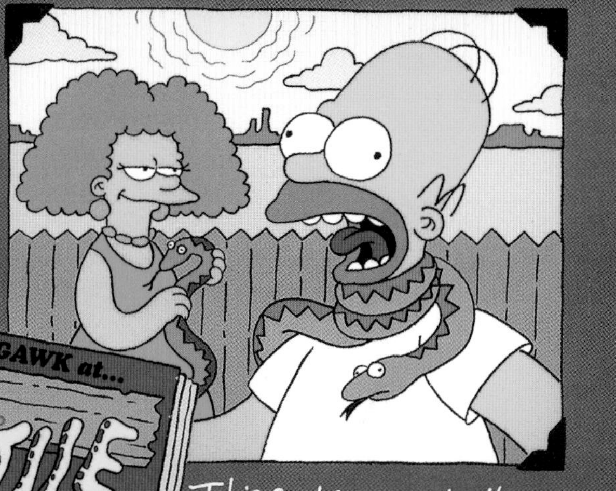

This snake was actually quite harmless. The proprietor explained he was just being "affectionate."

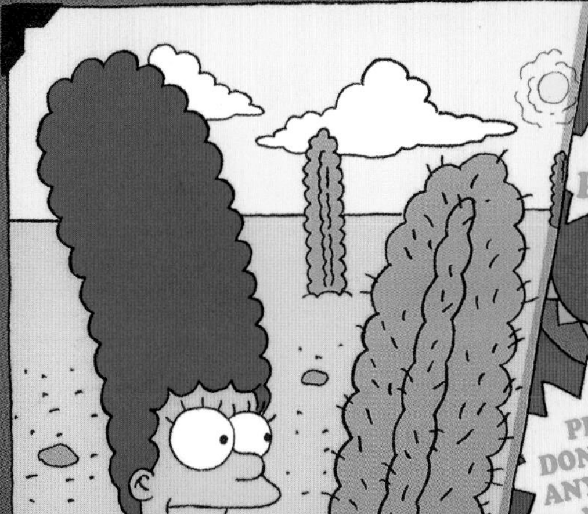

The Cacti of Mystery

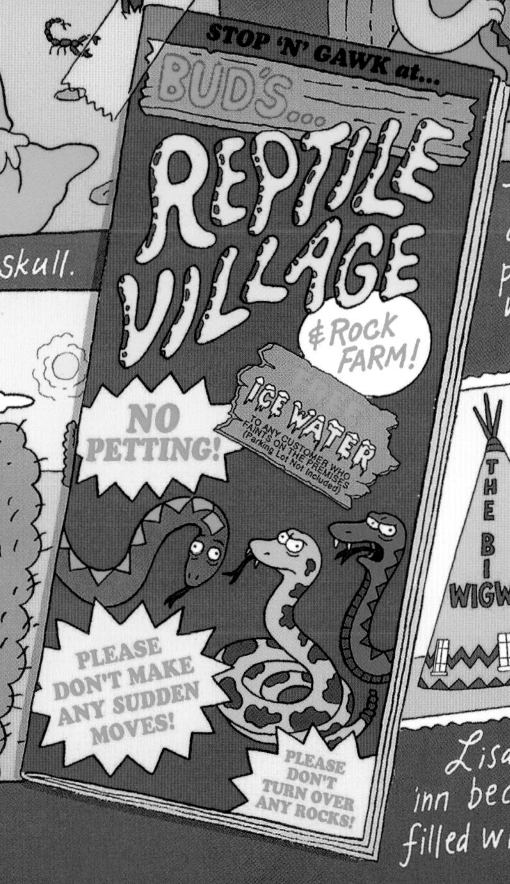
STOP 'N' GAWK at...
BUD'S...
REPTILE VILLAGE
& ROCK FARM!
FREE ICE WATER
TO ANY CUSTOMER WHO FAINTS ON THE PREMISES (Parking Lot Not Included)
NO PETTING!
PLEASE DON'T MAKE ANY SUDDEN MOVES!
PLEASE DON'T TURN OVER ANY ROCKS!

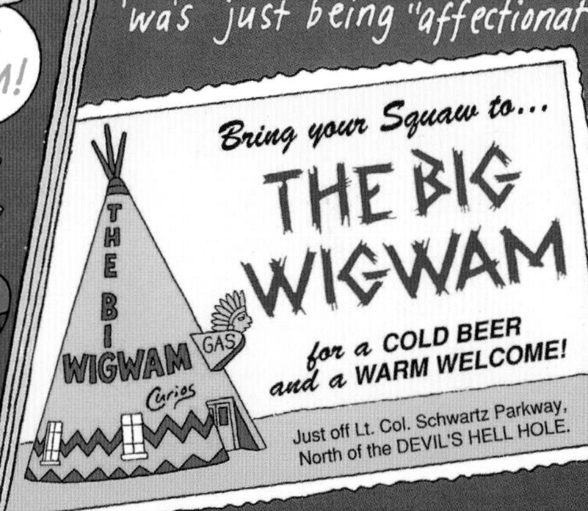
Bring your Squaw to...
THE BIG WIGWAM
for a COLD BEER and a WARM WELCOME!
Just off Lt. Col. Schwartz Parkway, North of the DEVIL'S HELL HOLE.
THE BIG
WIGWAM
GAS
Curios

Lisa loved this quaint roadside inn because they had a jukebox filled with scratchy old blues records.

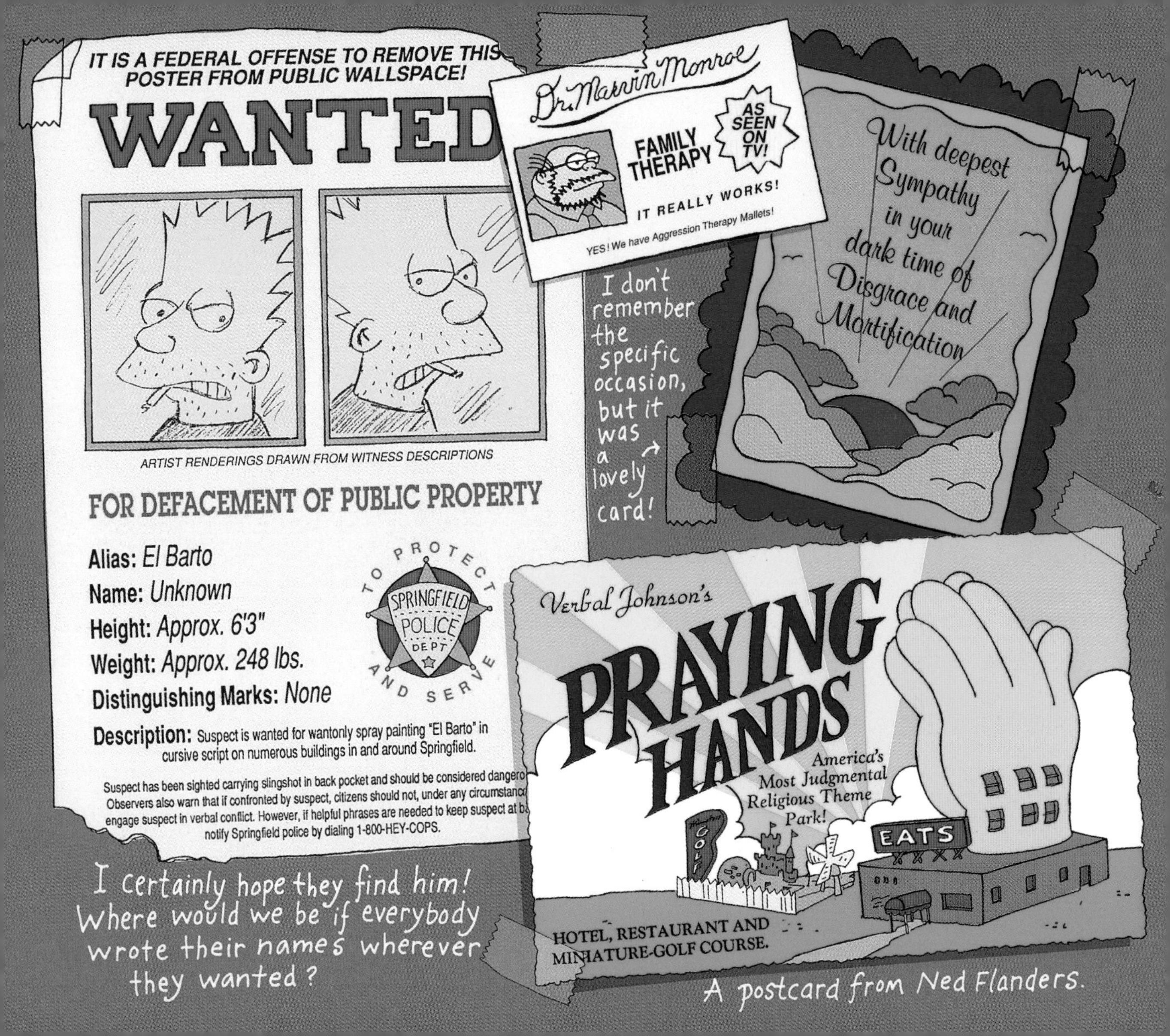
IT IS A FEDERAL OFFENSE TO REMOVE THIS POSTER FROM PUBLIC WALLSPACE!
WANTED
ARTIST RENDERINGS DRAWN FROM WITNESS DESCRIPTIONS
FOR DEFACEMENT OF PUBLIC PROPERTY
Alias: El Barto
Name: Unknown
Height: Approx. 6'3"
Weight: Approx. 248 lbs.
Distinguishing Marks: None
Description: Suspect is wanted for wantonly spray painting "El Barto" in cursive script on numerous buildings in and around Springfield.
Suspect has been sighted carrying slingshot in back pocket and should be considered dangero
Observers also warn that if confronted by suspect, citizens should not, under any circumstanc
engage suspect in verbal conflict. However, if helpful phrases are needed to keep suspect at b
notify Springfield police by dialing 1-800-HEY-COPS.
TO PROTECT AND SERVE
SPRINGFIELD POLICE DEPT
Dr. Marvin Monroe
FAMILY THERAPY
AS SEEN ON TV!
IT REALLY WORKS!
YES! We have Aggression Therapy Mallets!
With deepest Sympathy in your dark time of Disgrace and Mortification
I don't remember the specific occasion, but it was a lovely card!
Verbal Johnson's
PRAYING HANDS
America's Most Judgmental Religious Theme Park!
GOLF
EATS
HOTEL, RESTAURANT AND MINIATURE-GOLF COURSE.
I certainly hope they find him! Where would we be if everybody wrote their names wherever they wanted?
A postcard from Ned Flanders.

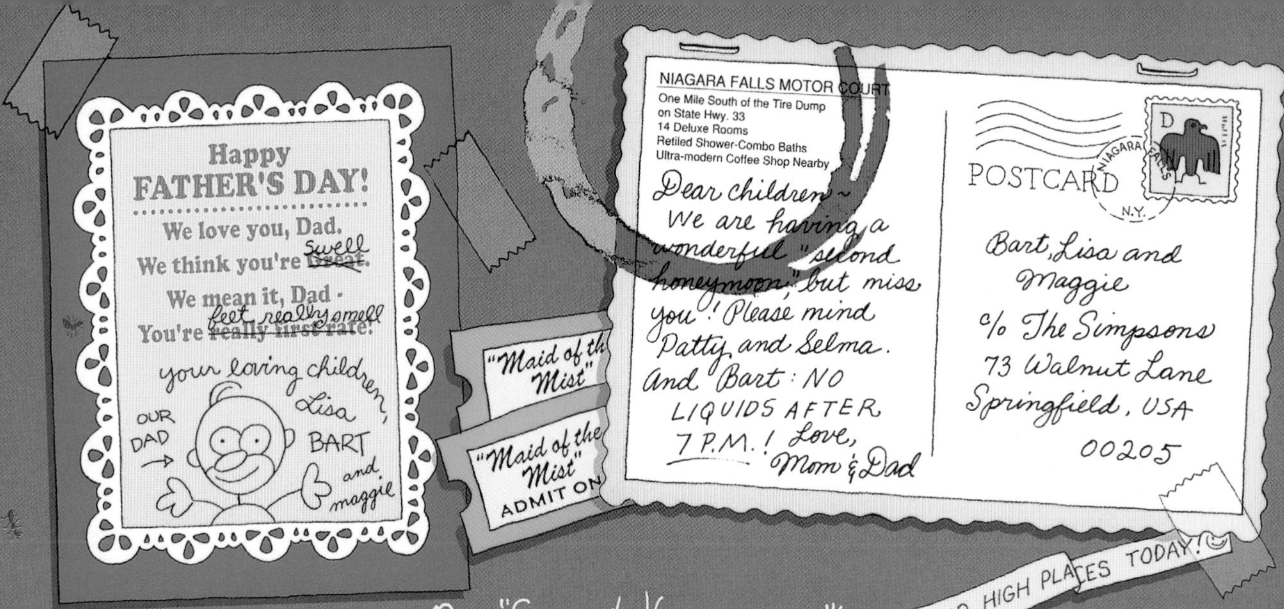
Happy
FATHER'S DAY!
We love you, Dad.
We think you're ~~Great~~ swell.
We mean it, Dad -
You're ~~really first rate~~ feet really smell.
your loving children,
Lisa
BART
and maggie
OUR DAD →
"Maid of th
Mist"
"Maid of the
Mist"
ADMIT ON
NIAGARA FALLS MOTOR COURT
One Mile South of the Tire Dump
on State Hwy. 33
14 Deluxe Rooms
Retiled Shower-Combo Baths
Ultra-modern Coffee Shop Nearby
Dear children ~
We are having a wonderful "second honeymoon," but miss you! Please mind Patty and Selma.
And Bart: NO LIQUIDS AFTER 7 P.M.! Love,
Mom & Dad
POSTCARD
NIAGARA FALLS N.Y.
D
Bart, Lisa and Maggie
c/o The Simpsons
73 Walnut Lane
Springfield, USA
00205
AVOID HIGH PLACES TODAY!

Our "Second Honeymoon"!

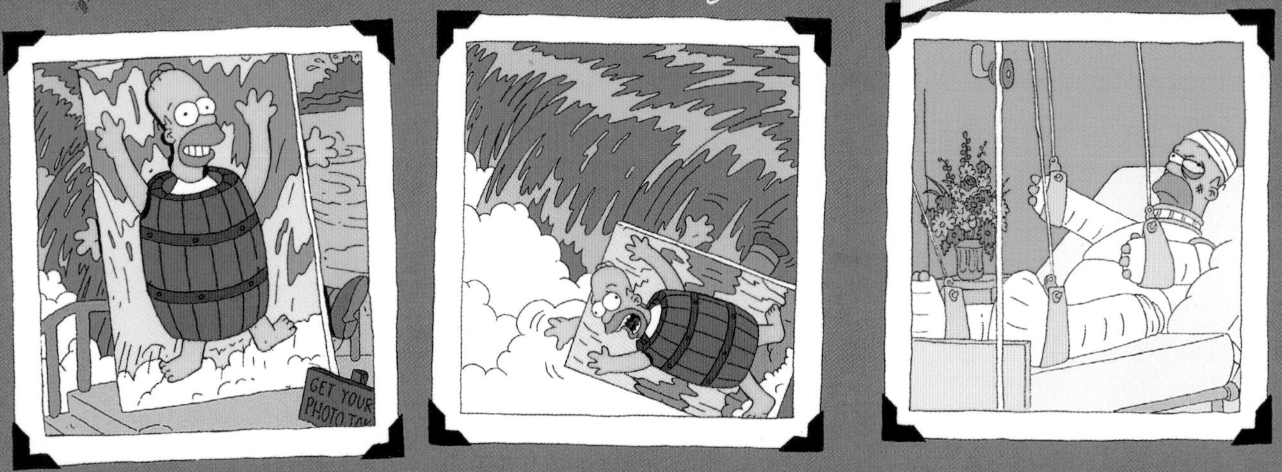
GET YOUR
PHOTO TA

(Cut short by a most unfortunate accident.)

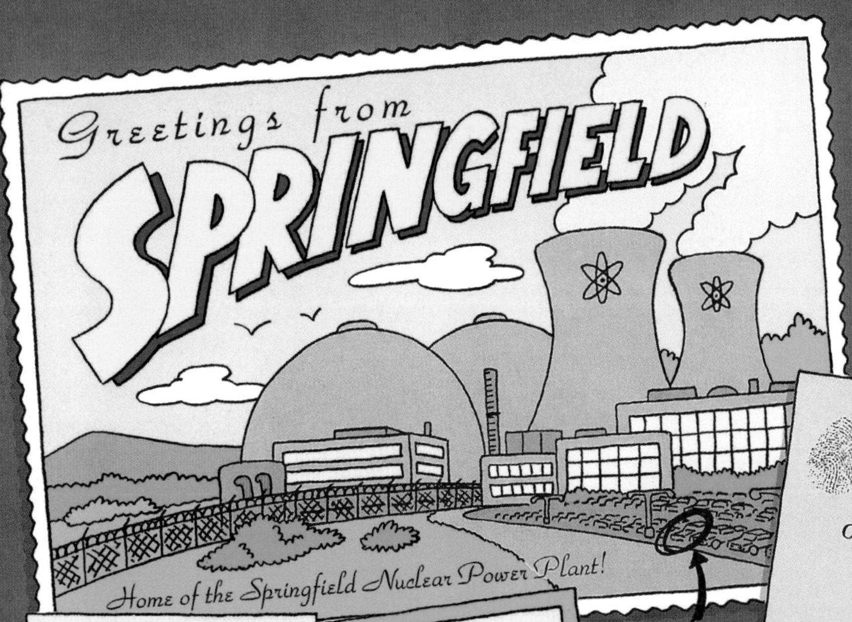

Greetings from
SPRINGFIELD
Home of the Springfield Nuclear Power Plant!


Homer's Car!

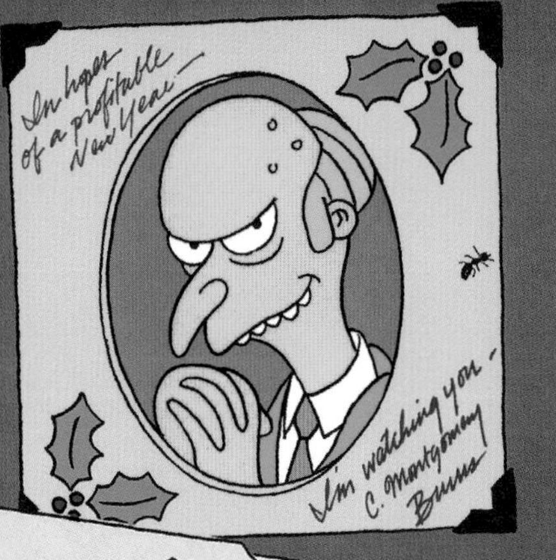

In hopes of a profitable New Year—
I'm watching you -
C. Montgomery Burns


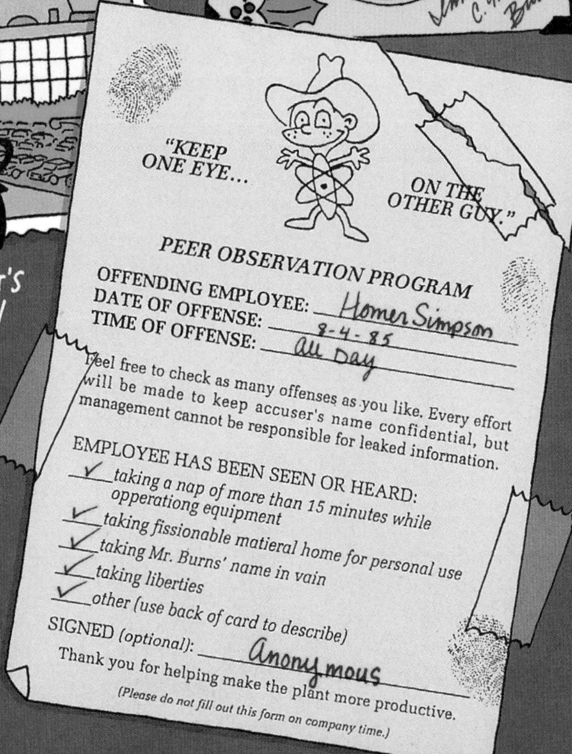

"KEEP ONE EYE...
ON THE OTHER GUY."


PEER OBSERVATION PROGRAM

OFFENDING EMPLOYEE: Homer Simpson
DATE OF OFFENSE: 8-4-85
TIME OF OFFENSE: All Day

Feel free to check as many offenses as you like. Every effort will be made to keep accuser's name confidential, but management cannot be responsible for leaked information.

EMPLOYEE HAS BEEN SEEN OR HEARD:

✓ *taking a nap of more than 15 minutes while operationg equipment*
✓ *taking fissionable matieral home for personal use*
✓ *taking Mr. Burns' name in vain*
✓ *taking liberties*
✓ *other (use back of card to describe)*

SIGNED *(optional)*: Anonymous

Thank you for helping make the plant more productive.

*(Please do not fill out this form on company time.)*

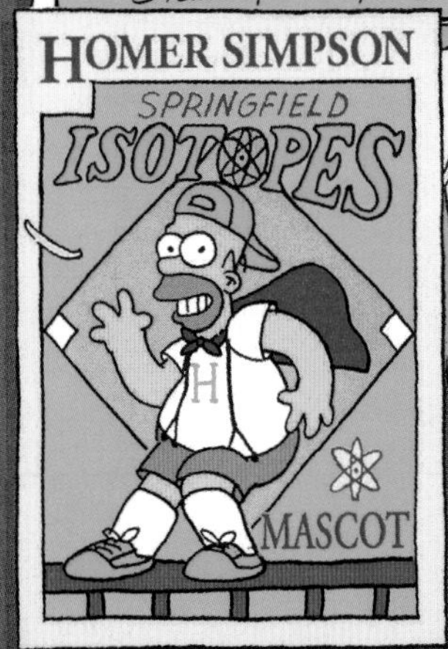

HOMER SIMPSON
SPRINGFIELD
ISOTOPES
MASCOT


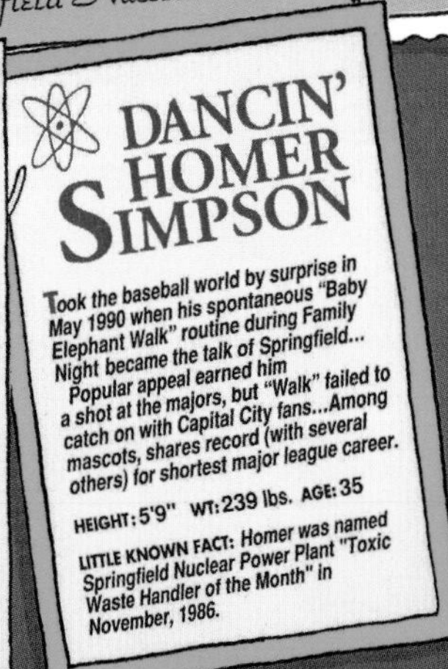

DANCIN' HOMER SIMPSON

Took the baseball world by surprise in May 1990 when his spontaneous "Baby Elephant Walk" routine during Family Night became the talk of Springfield... Popular appeal earned him a shot at the majors, but "Walk" failed to catch on with Capital City fans...Among mascots, shares record (with several others) for shortest major league career.

HEIGHT: 5'9" WT: 239 lbs. AGE: 35

LITTLE KNOWN FACT: Homer was named Springfield Nuclear Power Plant "Toxic Waste Handler of the Month" in November, 1986.

A Simpson on a trading card — I never thought I'd see the day!

The ticket Homer refused to pay. He said it was a "principal thing" and hung it on the refrigerator.

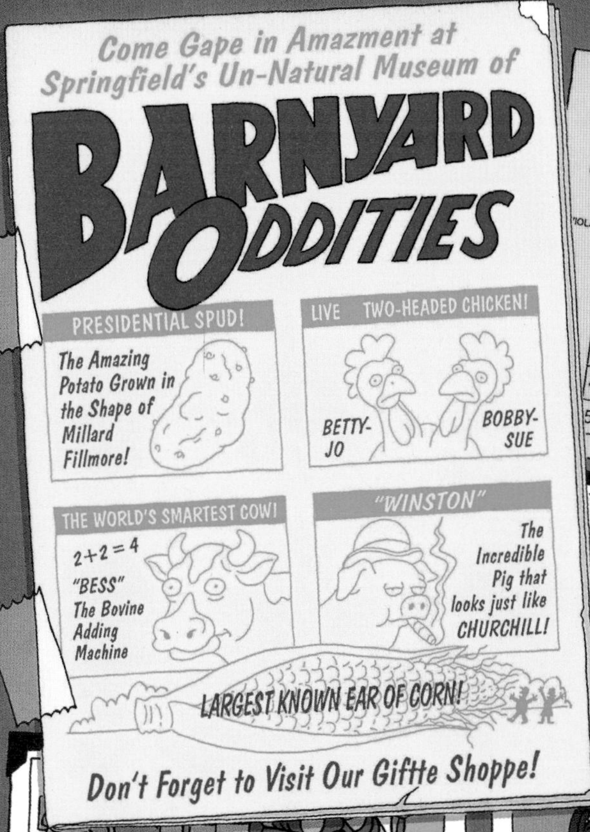
Come Gape in Amazment at Springfield's Un-Natural Museum of
BARNYARD ODDITIES
PRESIDENTIAL SPUD!
The Amazing Potato Grown in the Shape of Millard Fillmore!
LIVE TWO-HEADED CHICKEN!
BETTY-JO
BOBBY-SUE
THE WORLD'S SMARTEST COW!
2+2=4
"BESS" The Bovine Adding Machine
"WINSTON"
The Incredible Pig that looks just like CHURCHILL!
LARGEST KNOWN EAR OF CORN!
Don't Forget to Visit Our Giftte Shoppe!

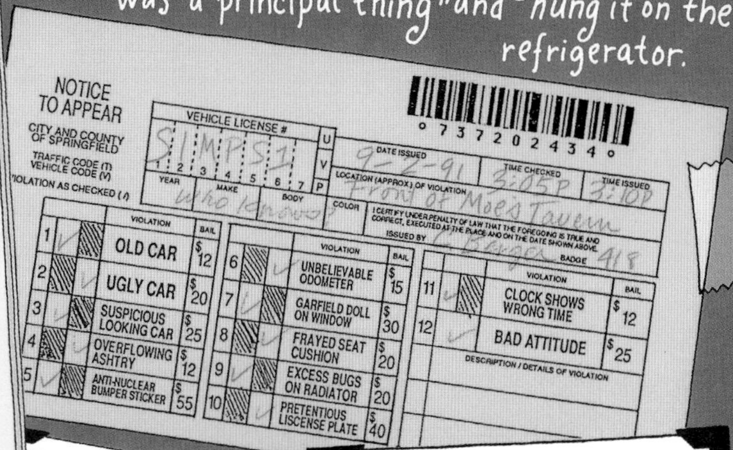

NOTICE TO APPEAR

CITY AND COUNTY OF SPRINGFIELD

TRAFFIC CODE (T)
VEHICLE CODE (V)
VIOLATION AS CHECKED (✓)

VEHICLE LICENSE #: SIMPS1

YEAR / MAKE / BODY: who knows?

0 7 3 7 2 0 2 4 3 4 0

DATE ISSUED: 9-2-91 | TIME CHECKED: 3:05P | TIME ISSUED: 3:10P

LOCATION (APPROX) OF VIOLATION: Front of Moe's Tavern

COLOR

I CERTIFY UNDER PENALTY OF LAW THAT THE FOREGOING IS TRUE AND CORRECT, EXECUTED AT THE PLACE AND ON THE DATE SHOWN ABOVE.

ISSUED BY: C. Barger BADGE: 418

| | VIOLATION | BAIL |
|---|---|---|
| 1 | OLD CAR | $12 |
| 2 | UGLY CAR | $20 |
| 3 | SUSPICIOUS LOOKING CAR | $25 |
| 4 | OVERFLOWING ASHTRY | $12 |
| 5 | ANTI-NUCLEAR BUMPER STICKER | $55 |
| 6 | UNBELIEVABLE ODOMETER | $15 |
| 7 | GARFIELD DOLL ON WINDOW | $30 |
| 8 | FRAYED SEAT CUSHION | $20 |
| 9 | EXCESS BUGS ON RADIATOR | $20 |
| 10 | PRETENTIOUS LISCENSE PLATE | $40 |
| 11 | CLOCK SHOWS WRONG TIME | $12 |
| 12 | BAD ATTITUDE | $25 |

DESCRIPTION / DETAILS OF VIOLATION

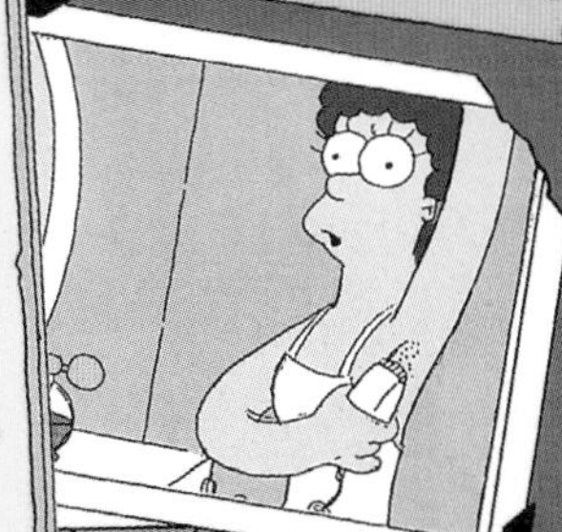

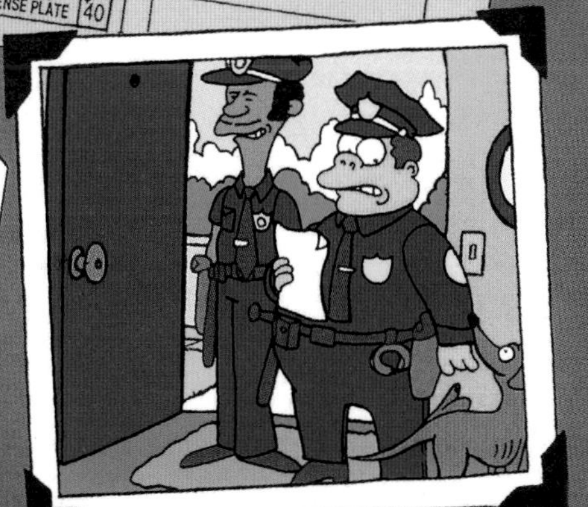

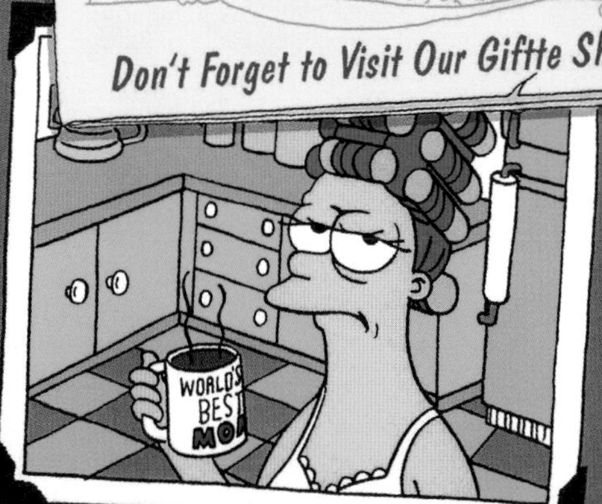
WORLD'S BEST MOM

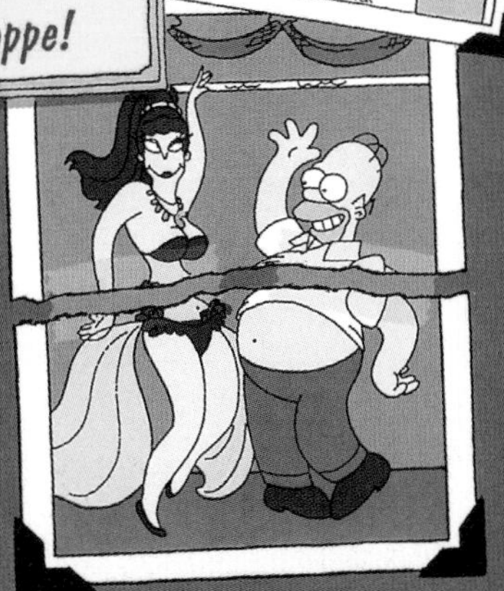

So later, Police Chief Wiggum and Eddie had to serve Homer with a warrant.

So much for matters of principal!

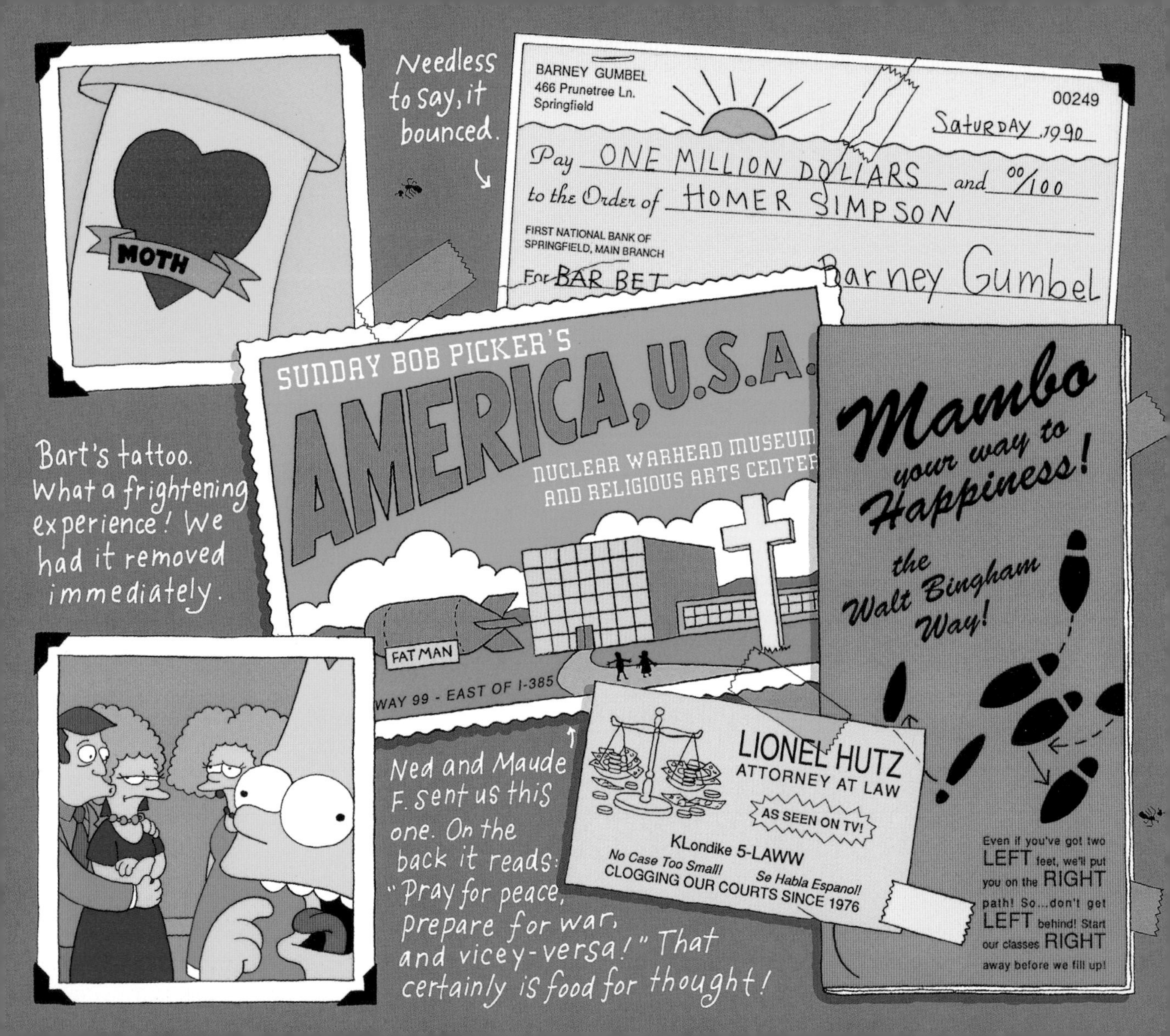
MOTH
Needless to say, it bounced.
BARNEY GUMBEL
466 Prunetree Ln.
Springfield
00249
Saturday, 1990
Pay ONE MILLION DOLLARS and 00/100
to the Order of HOMER SIMPSON
FIRST NATIONAL BANK OF SPRINGFIELD, MAIN BRANCH
For BAR BET
Barney Gumbel
Bart's tattoo. What a frightening experience! We had it removed immediately.
SUNDAY BOB PICKER'S
AMERICA, U.S.A.
NUCLEAR WARHEAD MUSEUM AND RELIGIOUS ARTS CENTER
FAT MAN
WAY 99 - EAST OF I-385
Mambo your way to Happiness!
the Walt Bingham Way!
Even if you've got two LEFT feet, we'll put you on the RIGHT path! So...don't get LEFT behind! Start our classes RIGHT away before we fill up!
LIONEL HUTZ
ATTORNEY AT LAW
AS SEEN ON TV!
KLondike 5-LAWW
No Case Too Small!
Se Habla Espanol!
CLOGGING OUR COURTS SINCE 1976
Ned and Maude F. sent us this one. On the back it reads: "Pray for peace, prepare for war, and vicey-versa!" That certainly is food for thought!

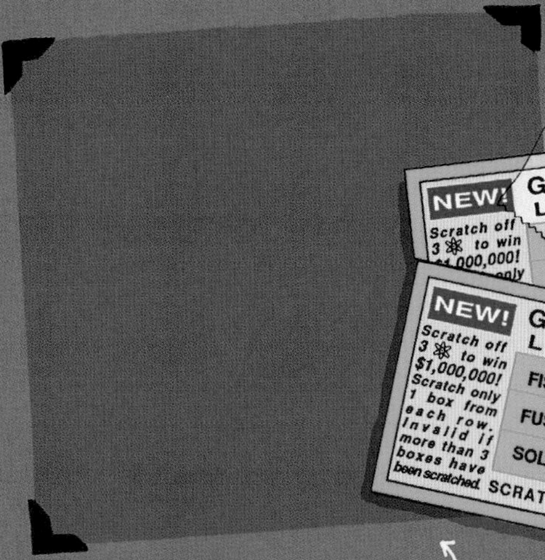

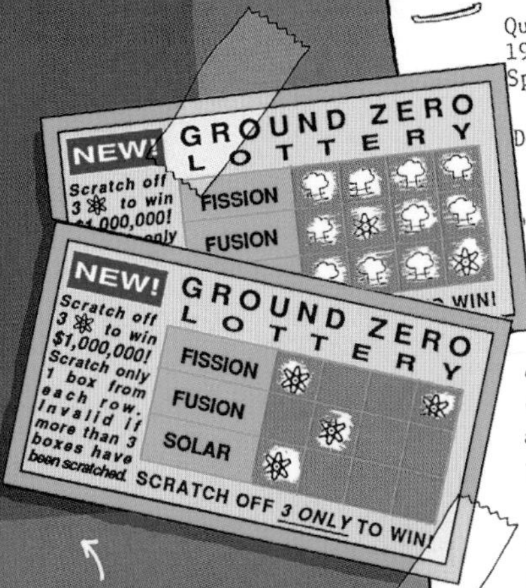
NEW!
GROUND ZERO LOTTERY
Scratch off 3 ⚛ to win $1,000,000!
FISSION
FUSION
WIN!
NEW!
GROUND ZERO LOTTERY
Scratch off 3 ⚛ to win $1,000,000! Scratch only 1 box from each row. Invalid if more than 3 boxes have been scratched.
FISSION
FUSION
SOLAR
SCRATCH OFF 3 ONLY TO WIN!

Bart naked on a bear skin rug.

Quality Candles
1954 Burns Parkway
Springfield

Dear Sir or Madam:

Correct me if I'm wrong, but I thought a person's 80th birthday was supposed to be a festive and dignified event.

I don't seem to hear you correcting me.

All right then, how do you suppose I felt when it was time to blow out the Quality (Hah! Now that's a hot one - if you get my meaning) Candle on my 80th birthday cake and I blew my damnedest and nothing happened. Oh, all right, maybe the flame did lean over a few degrees, but not so's you'd notice.

Tell me this, Mr. or Ms. rocket scientist. If I made a wish, and the candle didn't go out, do I get a bonus wish? Well, if I do, here it is: I wish your whole ball of wax would go up in smoke!

Smoldering mad,

Abraham Simpson

Abraham Simpson

P.S. Have you ever thought about making half-size birthday candles? It would save valuable time while honest people such as myself waited for the thing to burn to the ... And another thing - how about chocolate-flavored ... at pink stuff tastes awful!

EL BARTO WAS HERE

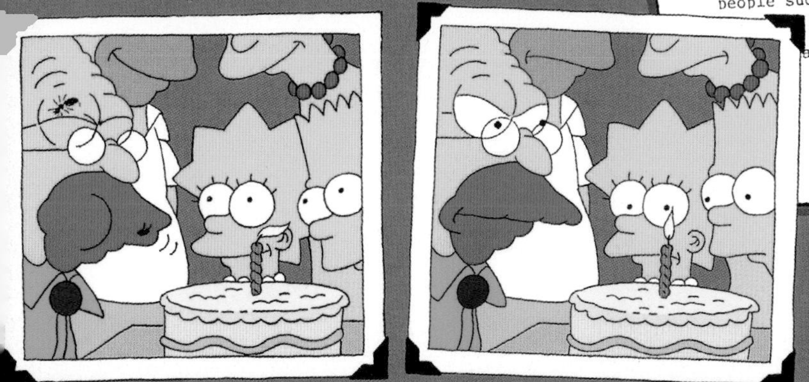

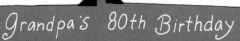

Grandpa's 80th Birthday

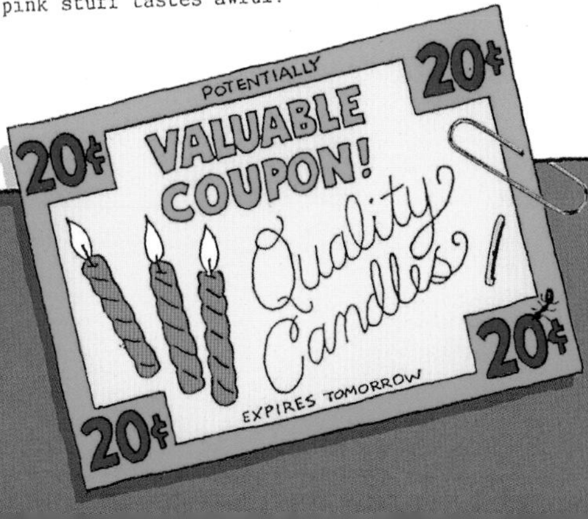
POTENTIALLY
VALUABLE COUPON!
Quality Candles
20¢
20¢
20¢
20¢
EXPIRES TOMORROW

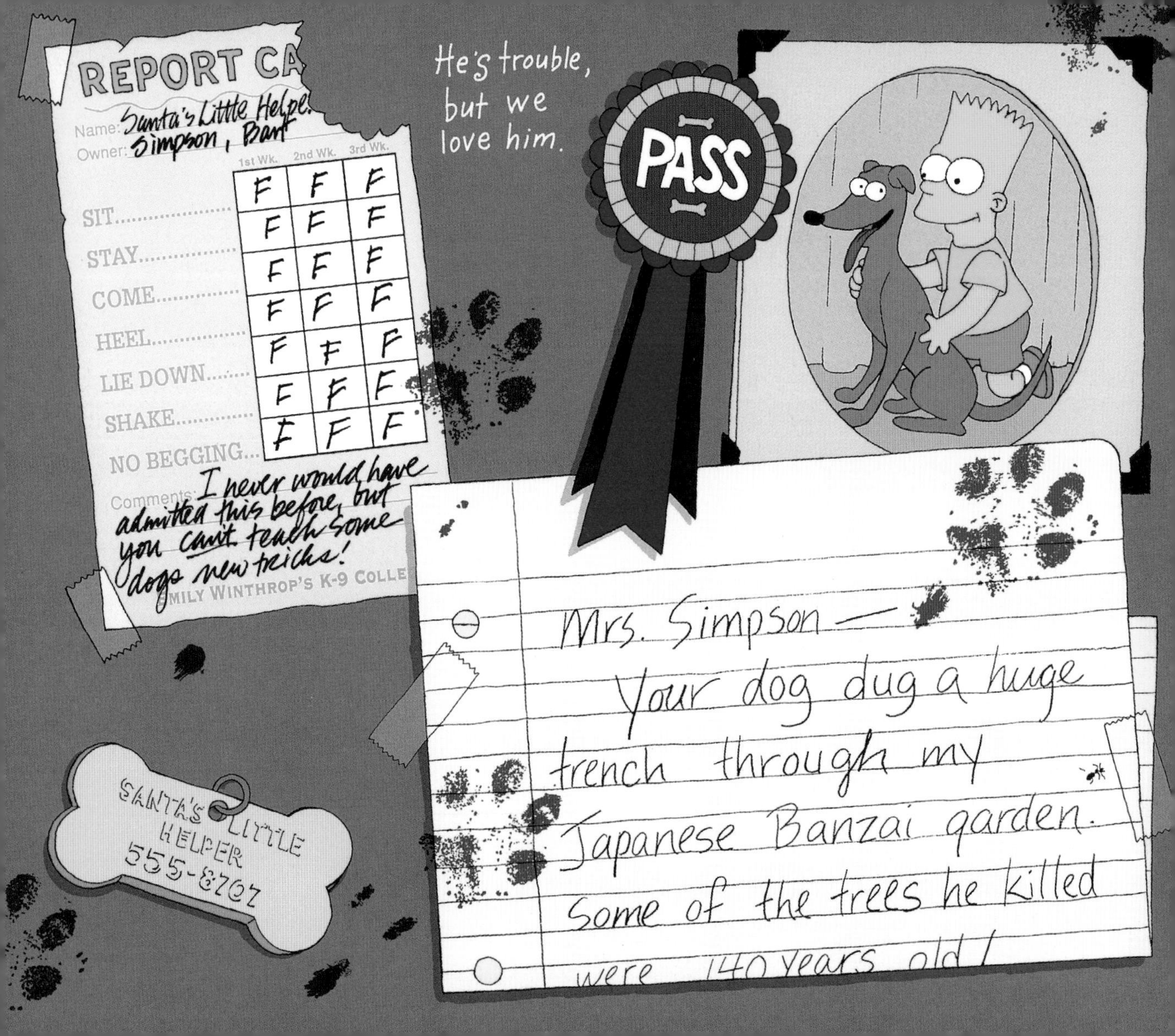
REPORT CA
Name: Santa's Little Helper
Owner: Simpson, Bart
1st Wk. 2nd Wk. 3rd Wk.
SIT F F F
STAY F F F
COME F F F
HEEL F F F
LIE DOWN F F F
SHAKE F F F
NO BEGGING F F F
Comments: I never would have admitted this before, but you can't teach some dogs new tricks!
EMILY WINTHROP'S K-9 COLLE
He's trouble, but we love him.
PASS
Mrs. Simpson —
Your dog dug a huge trench through my Japanese Banzai garden. Some of the trees he killed were 140 years old!
SANTA'S LITTLE HELPER
555-8707

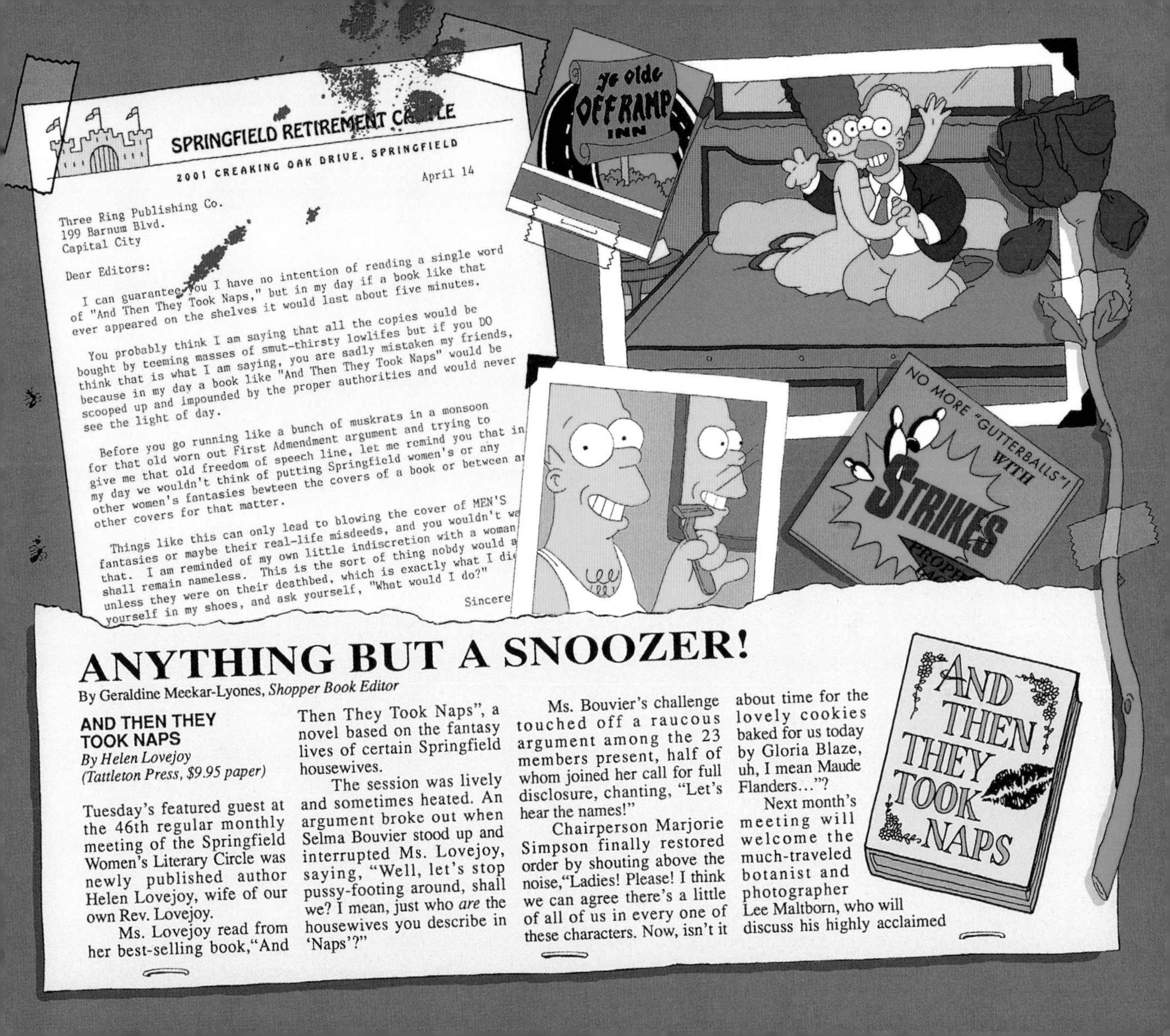

SPRINGFIELD RETIREMENT CASTLE

2001 CREAKING OAK DRIVE, SPRINGFIELD

April 14

Three Ring Publishing Co.
199 Barnum Blvd.
Capital City

Dear Editors:

I can guarantee you I have no intention of reading a single word of "And Then They Took Naps," but in my day if a book like that ever appeared on the shelves it would last about five minutes.

You probably think I am saying that all the copies would be bought by teeming masses of smut-thirsty lowlifes but if you DO think that is what I am saying, you are sadly mistaken my friends, because in my day a book like "And Then They Took Naps" would be scooped up and impounded by the proper authorities and would never see the light of day.

Before you go running like a bunch of muskrats in a monsoon for that old worn out First Admendment argument and trying to give me that old freedom of speech line, let me remind you that in my day we wouldn't think of putting Springfield women's or any other women's fantasies bewteen the covers of a book or between a other covers for that matter.

Things like this can only lead to blowing the cover of MEN'S fantasies or maybe their real-life misdeeds, and you wouldn't wa that. I am reminded of my own little indiscretion with a woman shall remain nameless. This is the sort of thing nobdy would a unless they were on their deathbed, which is exactly what I di yourself in my shoes, and ask yourself, "What would I do?"

Sincere


Ye Olde
OFF RAMP
INN
NO MORE "GUTTERBALLS"!
WITH
STRIKES
AND THEN THEY TOOK NAPS


# ANYTHING BUT A SNOOZER!

By Geraldine Meekar-Lyones, *Shopper Book Editor*

**AND THEN THEY TOOK NAPS**
*By Helen Lovejoy*
*(Tattleton Press, $9.95 paper)*

Tuesday's featured guest at the 46th regular monthly meeting of the Springfield Women's Literary Circle was newly published author Helen Lovejoy, wife of our own Rev. Lovejoy.

Ms. Lovejoy read from her best-selling book,"And Then They Took Naps", a novel based on the fantasy lives of certain Springfield housewives.

The session was lively and sometimes heated. An argument broke out when Selma Bouvier stood up and interrupted Ms. Lovejoy, saying, "Well, let's stop pussy-footing around, shall we? I mean, just who *are* the housewives you describe in 'Naps'?"

Ms. Bouvier's challenge touched off a raucous argument among the 23 members present, half of whom joined her call for full disclosure, chanting, "Let's hear the names!"

Chairperson Marjorie Simpson finally restored order by shouting above the noise,"Ladies! Please! I think we can agree there's a little of all of us in every one of these characters. Now, isn't it about time for the lovely cookies baked for us today by Gloria Blaze, uh, I mean Maude Flanders…"?

Next month's meeting will welcome the much-traveled botanist and photographer Lee Maltborn, who will discuss his highly acclaimed

## HOUSEWIFE WEEKLY

# Beauty Tips Contest!

SIMPLY FILL OUT THE FORM BELOW WITH ALL YOUR FAVORITE, TRIED-AND-TRUE BEAUTY SECRETS! WE ALL HAVE OUR LITTLE MIRACLE FORMULAS AND TOP-SECRET WRINKLE REMEDIES TO KEEP US LOOKING GOOD, SO WHY NOT SHARE YOURS?

1. To remove wrinkles, sleep with a yogurt facial treatment. BE sure to stir up fruit from bottom!
2. To make your eyes look bigger, curl lashes.
3. When in doubt about your hair, tease it!
4. Always clench your teeth when you smile.
5. Gravity is Beauty's enemy number one! Maintain bouyant thoughts
6. For younger-looking skin, lie face down in a mud puddle
7. for 20 minutes. Mix your base with orange food coloring for a more natural look.
8. Keep your hair looking peppy with static electricity!
9. Instead of drying your hair with a blow dryer, use a cotton candy machine.
10. My number one beauty se… a wo…

**YOU** COULD WIN AN ALL-EXPENSE PAID TRIP TO HOUSEWIFE WEEKLY'S BEAUTY HEAD-QUARTERS, A COMPLETE MAKE-OVER AND AN OPPORTUNITY TO BE A "BEFORE" AND "AFTER" MODEL IN THIS MAGAZINE!

Name Ma…
Address Walk…
Sprin…
Zip 00…
Phone 555…

I almost sent this in, but the idea of being a "before" just rubbed me the wrong way.

---

CT. 19 SPRINGFIELD SHO…

**LOST AND FOUND**

**LOST:** Maroon fez, size 3 7/8. Very rare, late 18th century Moroccan headgear. Owner heartsick. Personal identity at stake. REWARD. Contact Jeff at 555-3721.

**FOUND:** Flower pot-shaped object made of stiff, dark red felt. Seamless, with 8" black tassel attached to bottom. Object was left on bench near bulletin board at Springfield Natural Foods Collective. No reward expected, please. I'd just like to know what this thing is, what it's used for. Call 555-0463.

**MISSING**

Male cat and father of the offspring of Snowball II. Entire Family distraught. Children growing suspicious. Running out of excuses. If found, please contact the Simpsons at 555 - 8707.

**CLASSIFIED AN…**

**MEETINGS**

SPRINGFIELD SPRINGER SPANIEL SOCIETY meets third Wednesday of each month, Order of the Opossum Lodge basement. October 23, hear Lars Dengman, Universith of Malmo. Topic: "New Cholesterol-Free Doggie Donut Lite…Fetch or Forget?"

SPRINGFIELD CLASSICAL HUMMING CHORUS is looking for tenors. Ever find yourself just bursting into the Duh-duh-dun, duh-dun-dun, duh-duh-dun-dun-dun version of Rossini's "William Tell Overture"? Ever yearn to combine your talent with others? Then come to Room 222, Order of the Opossum Lodge, Wed. Oct.23. You could land a part in this year's humming of Holst's "The Planets"!

Something about the father's disappearance left me with an uneasy sense of déjà-vu.

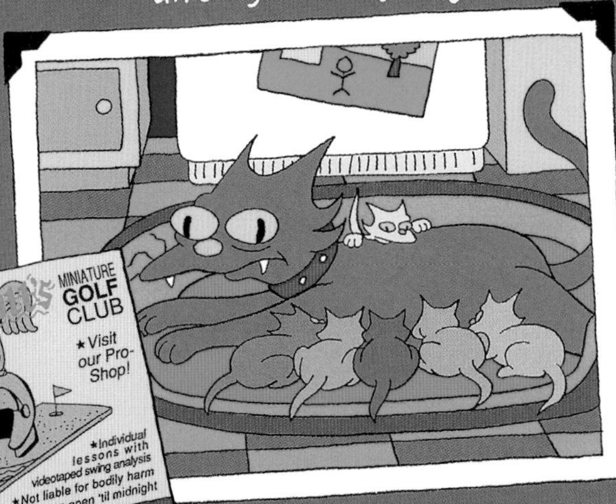

Snowball II, on the other hand, seemed completely unconcerned.

---

Sir Putt-A-Lot's MINIATURE GOLF CLUB

ALTERNATE SITE, 1995 U.S.M.G.A. SENIOR OPEN

13501 Burns Blvd.
Dial 555-FORE

★Visit our Pro-Shop!

★Individual lessons with videotaped swing analysis
★Not liable for bodily harm
★Putting range open 'til midnight

1 2 3 4 5 6 7 8 9 10

FULL BACK NINE WITH 10 FULL ROUNDS GOLF!

Lisa's second-grade play

Bart drew this at age seven...

# FEUD at SQUIRREL HOLLOW

## A PLAY IN TWO ACTS

Presented by the *Springfield Elementary Players*

| | |
|---|---|
| Grandma Checkerberry | Janey Hagstrom |
| Grandpa Checkerberry | Lewis Jackson |
| Lilly May | Susan Hegarty |
| Rufus | Robert DuRee |
| Ol' "Bugeared" Maloney | Frank Isola |
| Mayor Quimby | Lisa Simpson |
| | |
| Stage Hands | Bart Simpson |
| | Nelson Widmar |
| | |
| Lighting | Milhouse Light and Magic |
| Costumes | Carin Berger |
| Hair and Make-up | Terry Castillo |
| Directed by | Mrs.Hoover |

*ACT I:* The fur flies when Grandma finds her *go-to-meetin'* dress full of buckshot holes. On Grandpa's advice, she suspects Rufus and tells him so, but Rufus has a darn good alibi. Together, Grandma, Grandpa and Rufus vow to get to the bottom of this.

*ACT II:* The trail leads straight to Ol' Bugeared Maloney–or does it? Turns out he's got a darn good alibi too. Ol' Bugeared joins the posse, and the four vigilantes keep trying to get to the bottom of this. Finally...Eureka! (Hang onto your seats.)

She was so proud to be cast as the Mayor!

MY DAD

BART

Not a bad likeness, really.

Bart was in charge of lighting

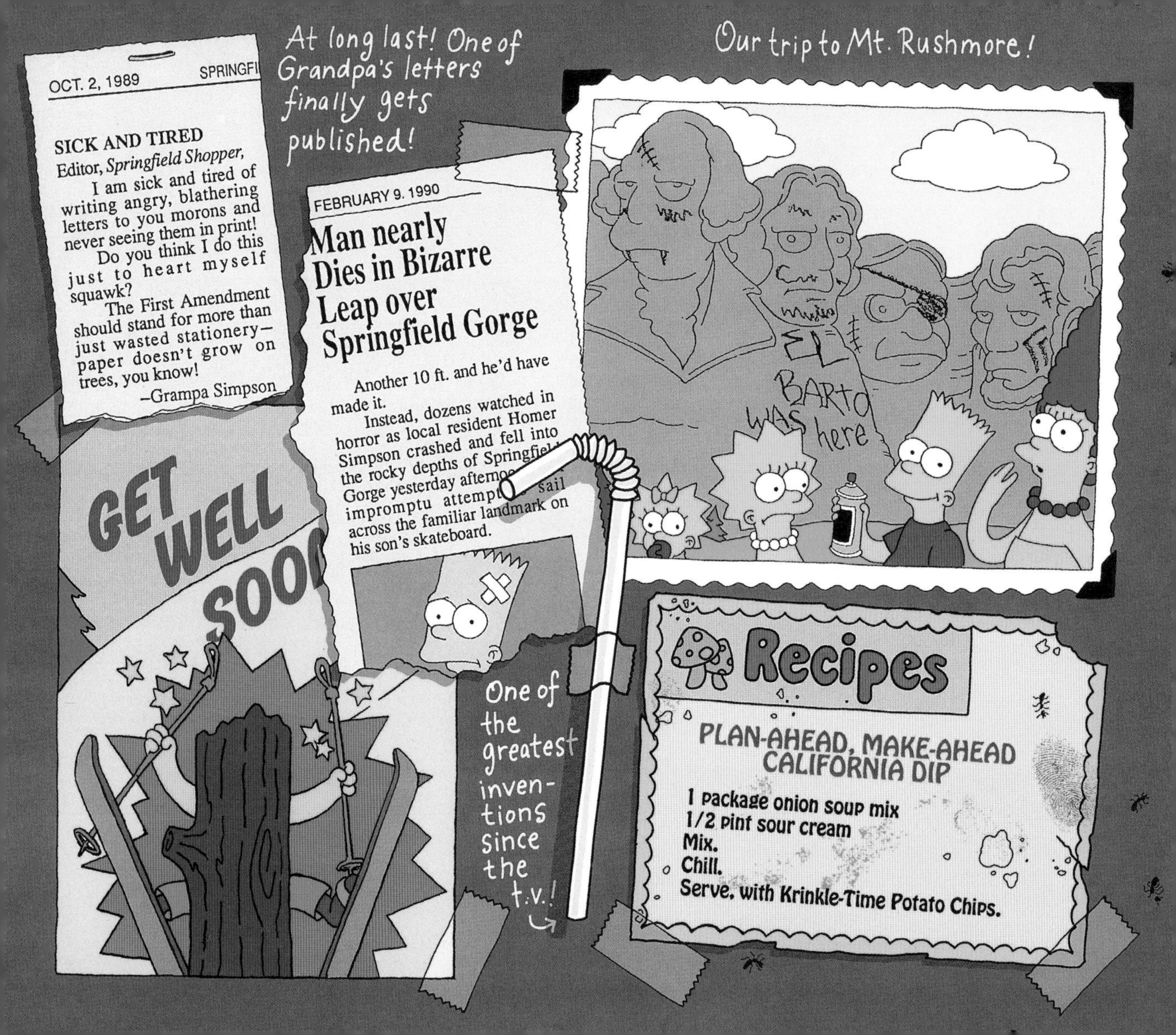
At long last! One of Grandpa's letters finally gets published!
OCT. 2, 1989
SPRINGFI
SICK AND TIRED
Editor, Springfield Shopper,
I am sick and tired of writing angry, blathering letters to you morons and never seeing them in print!
Do you think I do this just to heart myself squawk?
The First Amendment should stand for more than just wasted stationery—paper doesn't grow on trees, you know!
–Grampa Simpson
FEBRUARY 9. 1990
Man nearly Dies in Bizarre Leap over Springfield Gorge
Another 10 ft. and he'd have made it.
Instead, dozens watched in horror as local resident Homer Simpson crashed and fell into the rocky depths of Springfiel Gorge yesterday afternoo sail impromptu attempt across the familiar landmark on his son's skateboard.
GET WELL SOO
Our trip to Mt. Rushmore!
EL
BART
WAS here
One of the greatest inventions since the t.v.!
Recipes
PLAN-AHEAD, MAKE-AHEAD CALIFORNIA DIP
1 package onion soup mix
1/2 pint sour cream
Mix.
Chill.
Serve, with Krinkle-Time Potato Chips.

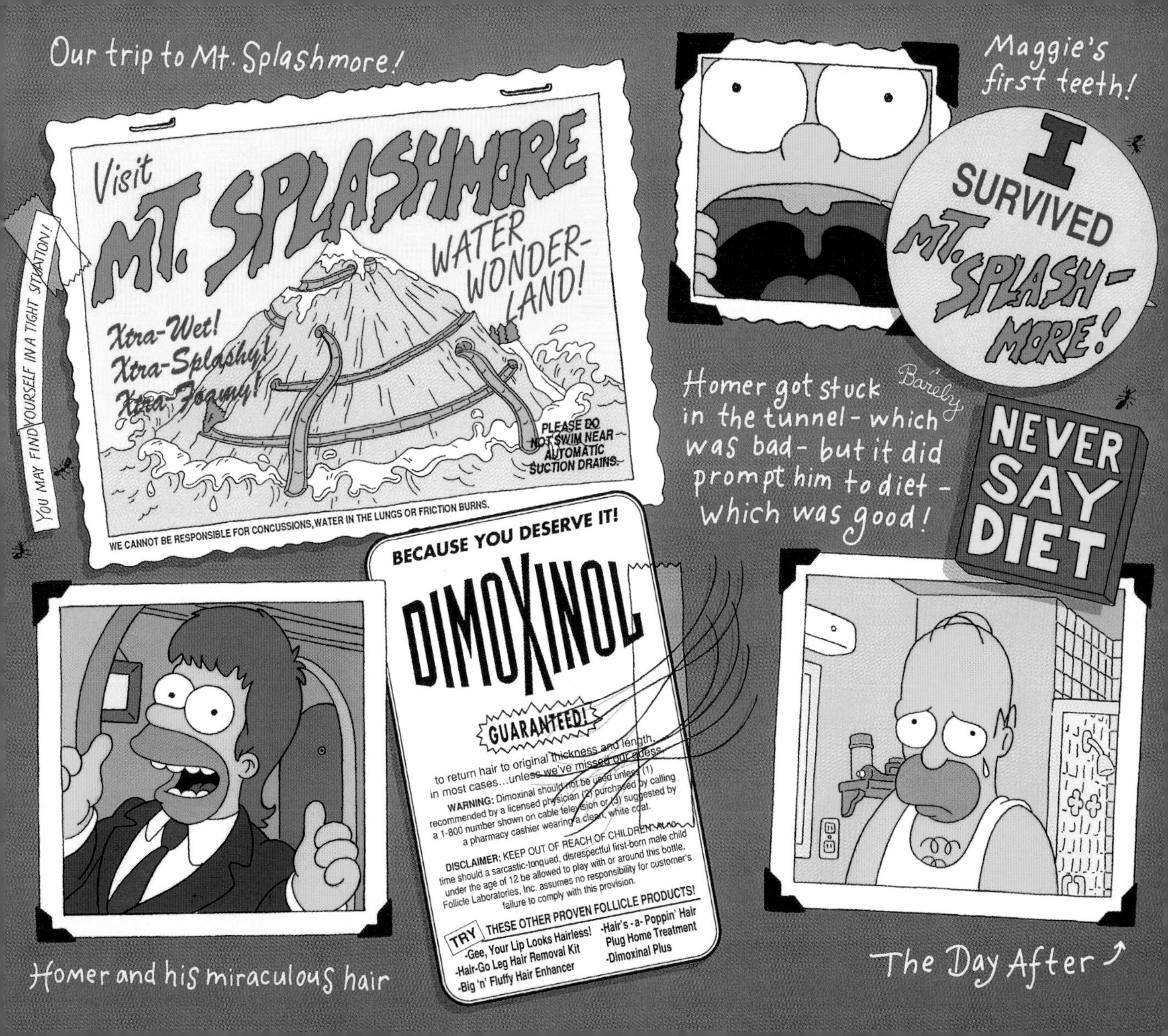

Our trip to Mt. Splashmore!
Visit
MT. SPLASHMORE
WATER WONDER-LAND!
Xtra-Wet!
Xtra-Splashy!
Xtra-Foamy!
PLEASE DO NOT SWIM NEAR AUTOMATIC SUCTION DRAINS.
WE CANNOT BE RESPONSIBLE FOR CONCUSSIONS, WATER IN THE LUNGS OR FRICTION BURNS.
YOU MAY FIND YOURSELF IN A TIGHT SITUATION!
Maggie's first teeth!
I SURVIVED MT. SPLASH-MORE!
Barely
Homer got stuck in the tunnel - which was bad - but it did prompt him to diet - which was good!
NEVER SAY DIET
BECAUSE YOU DESERVE IT!
DIMOXINOL
GUARANTEED!
to return hair to original thickness and length, in most cases…unless we've missed our guess.
WARNING: Dimoxinal should not be used unless (1) recommended by a licensed physician (2) purchased by calling a 1-800 number shown on cable television or (3) suggested by a pharmacy cashier wearing a clean, white coat.
DISCLAIMER: KEEP OUT OF REACH OF CHILDREN. At no time should a sarcastic-tongued, disrespectful first-born male child under the age of 12 be allowed to play with or around this bottle. Follicle Laboratories, Inc. assumes no responsibility for customer's failure to comply with this provision.
TRY THESE OTHER PROVEN FOLLICLE PRODUCTS!
-Gee, Your Lip Looks Hairless!
-Hair-Go Leg Hair Removal Kit
-Big 'n' Fluffy Hair Enhancer
-Hair's - a - Poppin' Hair Plug Home Treatment
-Dimoxinal Plus
Homer and his miraculous hair
The Day After

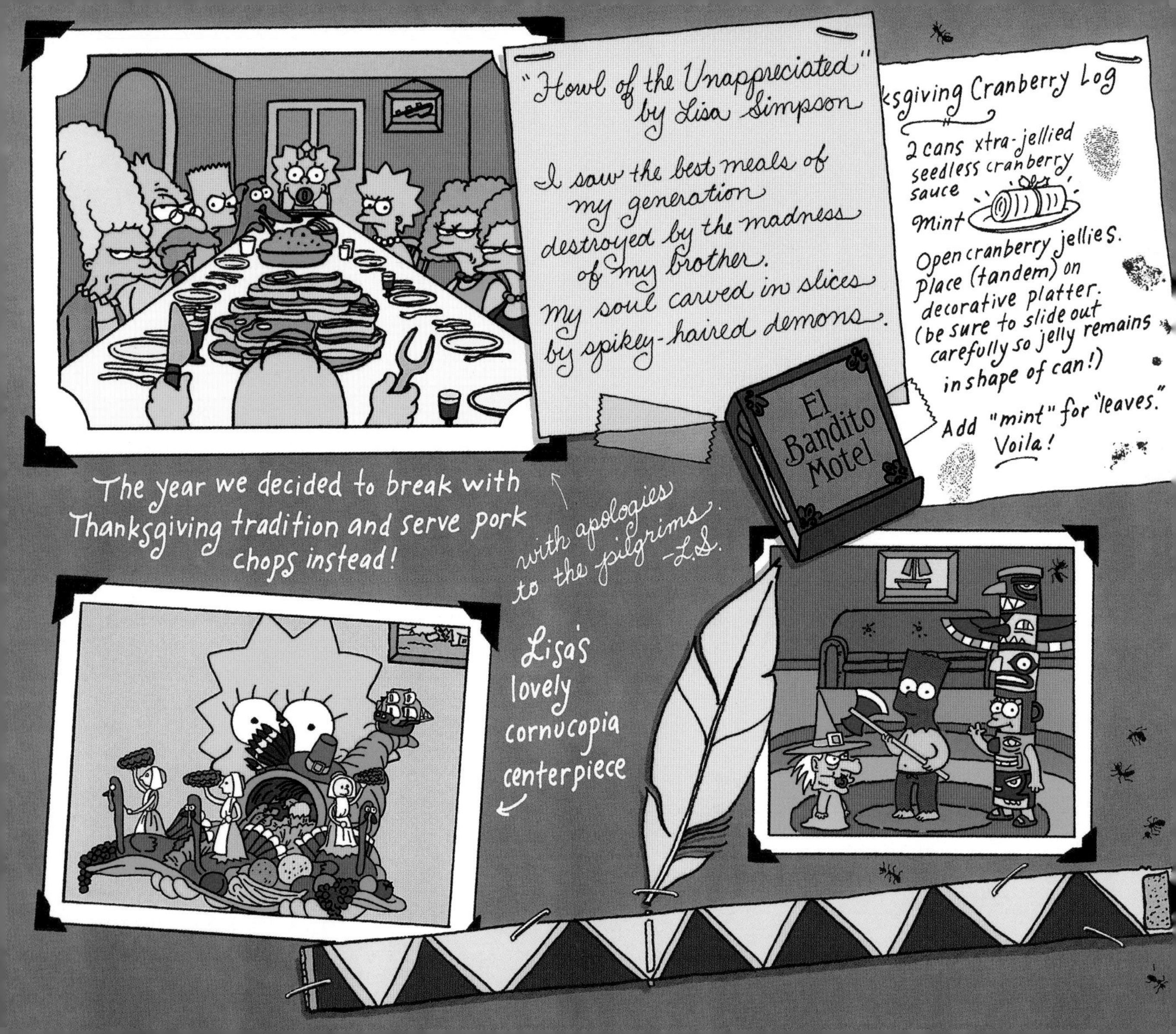
"Howl of the Unappreciated"
by Lisa Simpson
I saw the best meals of
my generation
destroyed by the madness
of my brother.
My soul carved in slices
by spikey-haired demons.
ksgiving Cranberry Log
2 cans xtra-jellied seedless cranberry sauce
Mint
Open cranberry jellies.
Place (tandem) on decorative platter.
(be sure to slide out carefully so jelly remains in shape of can!)
Add "mint" for "leaves."
Voila!
El Bandito Motel
The year we decided to break with Thanksgiving tradition and serve pork chops instead!
with apologies to the pilgrims. -L.S.
Lisa's lovely cornucopia centerpiece

Dear Principal Skinne
Please excuse Bart's
absince from school
~~today~~, March 3-5. He
stayed home to take
care of his mother,
who could not use her
hands because she
burned both of them
in a Terrible Kitchen
accident, which is
why this letter looks
like a kid did it.

Sincerely,
Margorie Simpson
March 6th

SPRINGFIELD ELEMENTARY SCHOOL

March 6

Dear Mr. and Mrs. Simpson:

I know I've said this many times before, but this really is the last straw.

Enclosed you will find your son Bartholomew's latest pathetic attempt at forgery. If he thinks he can hoodwink my authority, he's got another think coming.

I'm afraid your son Bartholomew is on a one-way conveyor belt to J.D.H., and I don't mean the Junior Disneyland Hotel. I mean the Juvenile Detention Home!

I am adding another 40 days detention, which brings his total to 462 days.

He will also be required to write on the blackboard 1000 times:

A FORGED EXCUSE IS INEXCUSABLE.

I can only hope you will take even sterner measures of discipline in the privacy of your own home.

Sincerely,

Seymour Skinner

Seymour Skinner
Principal

SPRINGFIELD ELEME

# REPORT CARD

SPRINGFIELD ELEMENTARY SCHOOL

ent: Simpson, Bart

| | 1st SEM. | 2nd SEM. | 3rd SEM. |
|---|---|---|---|
| Arithmatic | F | D- | F |
| Social Studies | D+ | F | F+ |
| English | D- | F+ | D |
| History | F | F | D- |
| Art | F- | D | D+ |
| P.E. | D+ | F | F |

omments: Dear Mr. and Mrs. Simpson,
As we are painfully aware, Bart is his own worst enemy.
Unfortunately, the enemy is winning.
Nothing you or I could say or do would make a bit of difference.
With mutual concern,
Ms. Krabappel

***From the Desk of***

**J. Loren Pryor**
DISTRICT PSYCHOLOGIST

SUBJECT: Bart Simpson Age: 10

EVALUATION: Subject exhibits need to draw excessive attention to himself. Confrontational behavior includes attempts at raw humor intended to confuse authority figures and disrupt peer group order.

CONCLUSION: Rotten Little Punk.

SIGNED: J. Loren Pryor

EL
BARTO
WAS
HERE

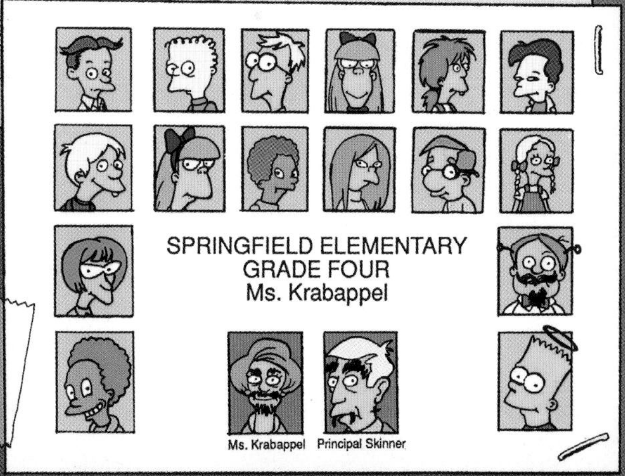

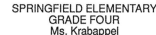

SPRINGFIELD ELEMENTARY
GRADE FOUR
Ms. Krabappel
Ms. Krabappel
Principal Skinner

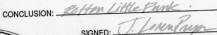

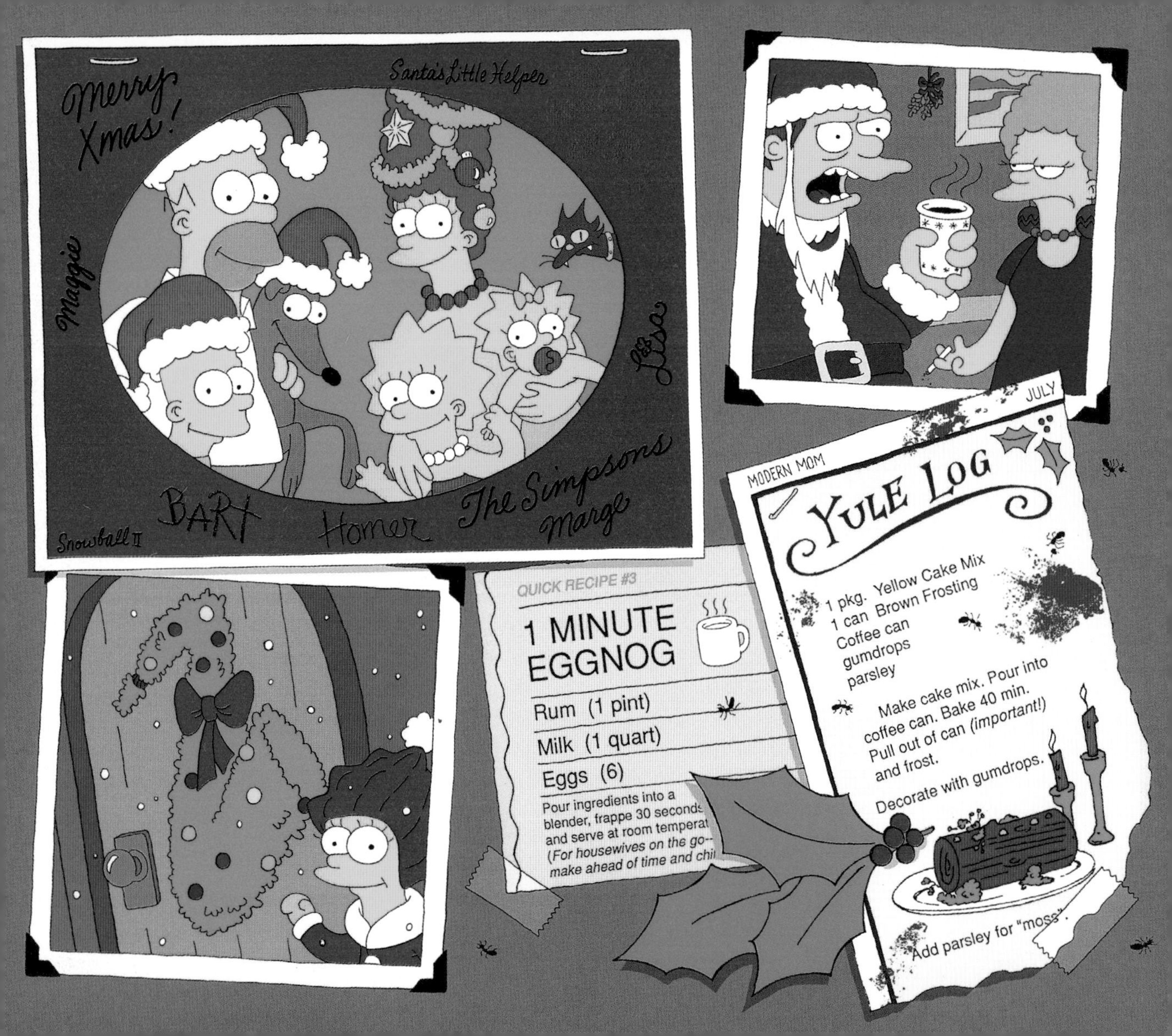
Merry Xmas!
Santa's Little Helper
Maggie
Lisa
The Simpsons
BART
Homer
marge
Snowball II
QUICK RECIPE #3
1 MINUTE EGGNOG
Rum (1 pint)
Milk (1 quart)
Eggs (6)
Pour ingredients into a blender, frappe 30 seconds and serve at room temperat
(For housewives on the go-- make ahead of time and chi
MODERN MOM
JULY
YULE LOG
1 pkg. Yellow Cake Mix
1 can Brown Frosting
Coffee can
gumdrops
parsley
Make cake mix. Pour into coffee can. Bake 40 min. Pull out of can (important!) and frost.
Decorate with gumdrops.
Add parsley for "moss".

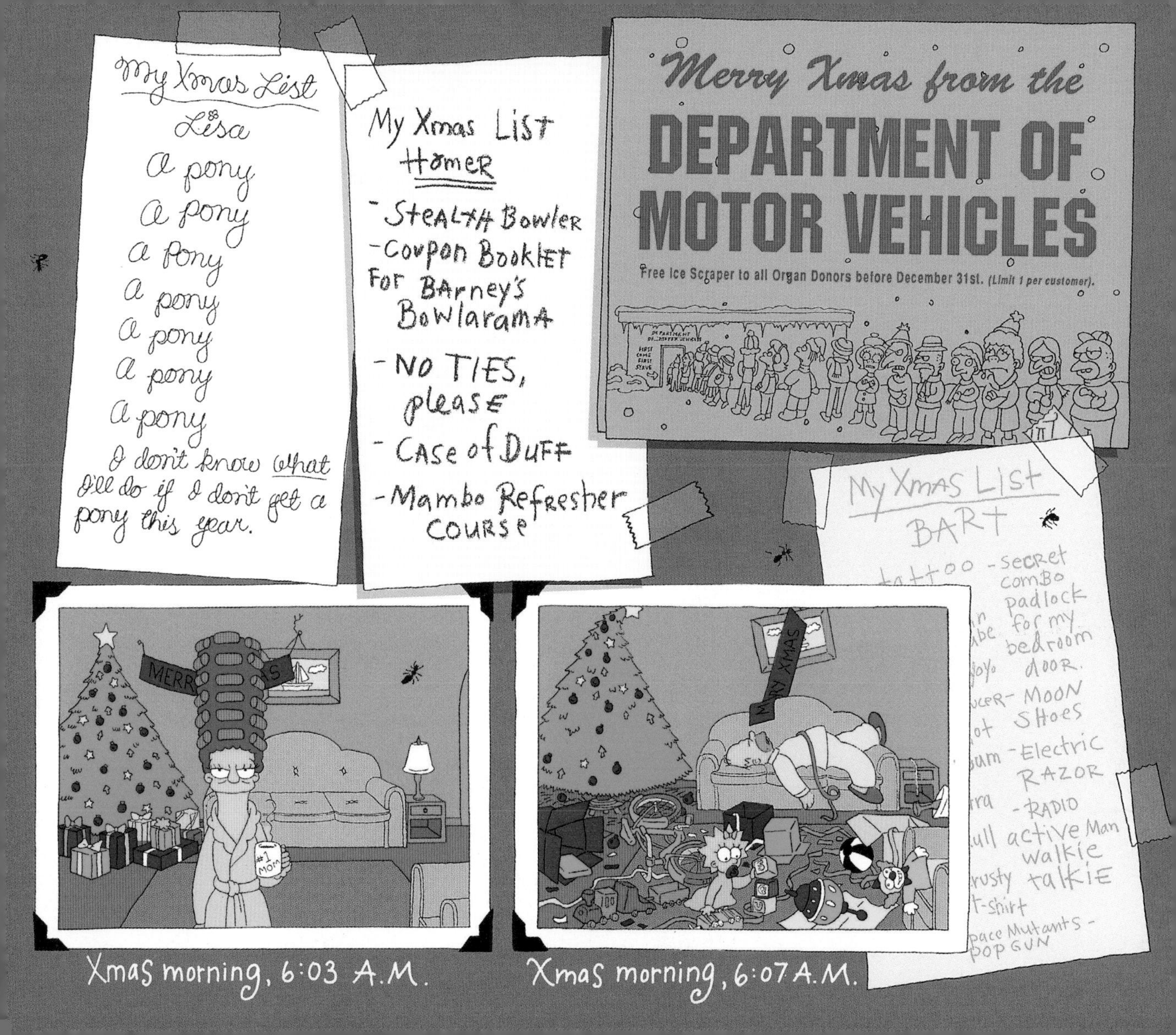
My Xmas List
Lisa
A pony
A pony
A Pony
A pony
A pony
A pony
A pony
I don't know what I'll do if I don't get a pony this year.
My Xmas LIST
Homer
- Stealth Bowler
- Coupon Booklet For Barney's Bowlarama
- NO TIES, please
- Case of Duff
- Mambo Refresher course
Merry Xmas from the
DEPARTMENT OF MOTOR VEHICLES
Free Ice Scraper to all Organ Donors before December 31st. (Limit 1 per customer).
DEPARTMENT OF MOTOR VEHICLES
FIRST COME FIRST SERVE
My Xmas List
BART
tattoo
-secret combo padlock for my bedroom door.
yoyo
- MOON SHOES
- Electric RAZOR
- RADIO
active Man walkie talkie
t-shirt
pace Mutants - POP GUN
MERR
#1 MOM
MERRY XMAS
Xmas morning, 6:03 A.M.
Xmas morning, 6:07 A.M.

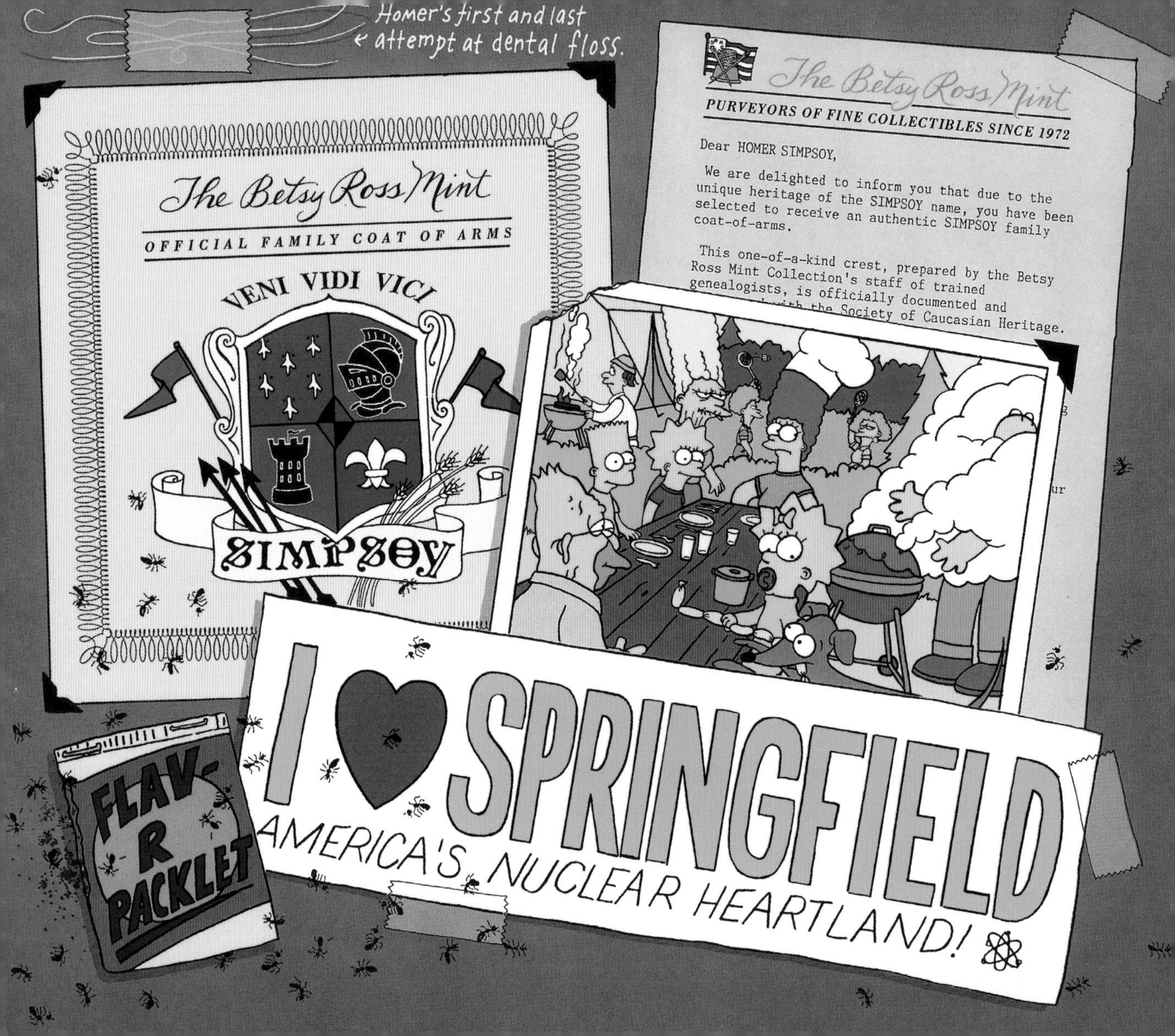

Homer's first and last
← attempt at dental floss.
The Betsy Ross Mint
OFFICIAL FAMILY COAT OF ARMS
VENI VIDI VICI
SIMPSOY
The Betsy Ross Mint
PURVEYORS OF FINE COLLECTIBLES SINCE 1972
Dear HOMER SIMPSOY,
We are delighted to inform you that due to the unique heritage of the SIMPSOY name, you have been selected to receive an authentic SIMPSOY family coat-of-arms.
This one-of-a-kind crest, prepared by the Betsy Ross Mint Collection's staff of trained genealogists, is officially documented and
with the Society of Caucasian Heritage.
FLAV-R PACKLET
I ♥ SPRINGFIELD
AMERICA'S NUCLEAR HEARTLAND!

Dear Memory Book--

Well, there you have us--the Simpsons in a nutshell. We've had some laughs, we've had some tears, we've had some bruises, we've had some nasty sprains. But all in all, looking back on everything, I just sit here in wonder that we Simpsons are somehow a part of God's mysterious plan... If the song is right, and life is but a dream, I can only hope I never wake up.

Cordially yours,

Marge Simpson

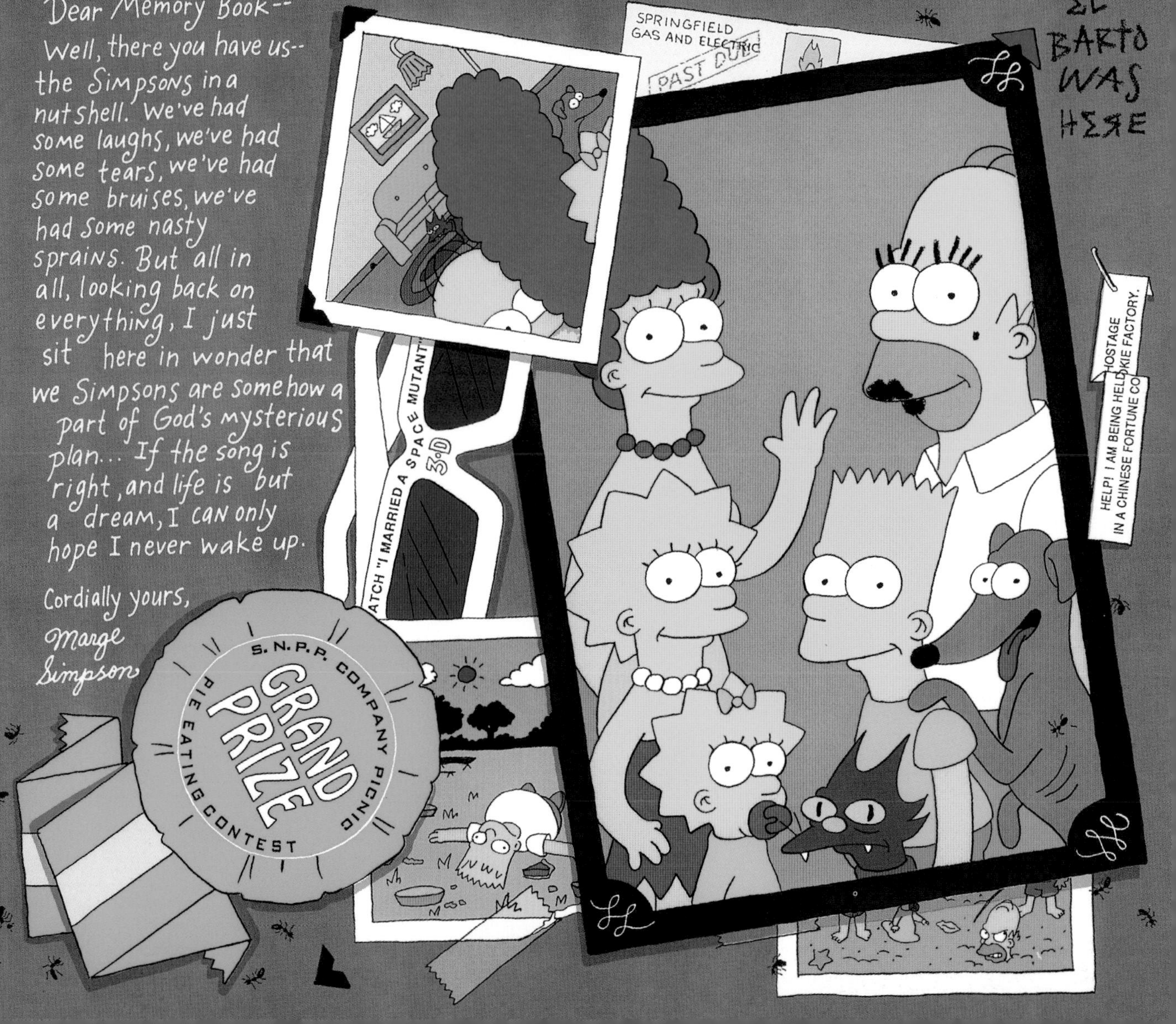
SPRINGFIELD GAS AND ELECTRIC
PAST DUE
EL BARTO WAS HERE
HELP! I AM BEING HELD HOSTAGE IN A CHINESE FORTUNE CO KIE FACTORY.
ATCH "I MARRIED A SPACE MUTANT" 3-D
S.N.P.P. COMPANY PICNIC
GRAND PRIZE
PIE EATING CONTEST

Dedicated to the memory of
Snowball I:

We've re-upholstered the couch you shredded,
but not our love for you.

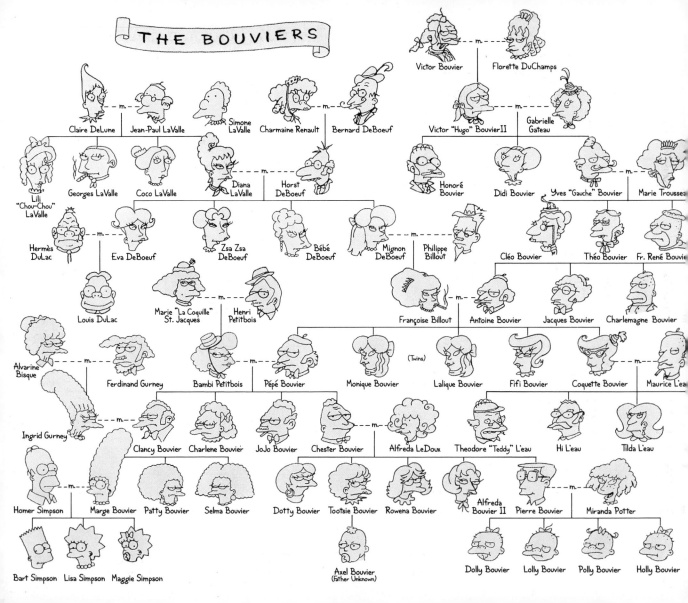

# THE BOUVIERS

Victor Bouvier - m. - Florette DuChamps

Claire DeLune - m. - Jean-Paul LaValle    Simone LaValle    Charmaine Renault - m. - Bernard DeBoeuf

Victor "Hugo" Bouvier II - m. - Gabrielle Gateau

Lili "Chou-Chou" LaValle    Georges LaValle    Coco LaValle    Diana LaValle - m. - Horst DeBoeuf

Honoré Bouvier    Didi Bouvier    Yves "Gauche" Bouvier - m. - Marie Trousseau

Hermès DuLac - m. - Eva DeBoeuf    Zsa Zsa DeBoeuf    Bébé DeBoeuf    Mignon DeBoeuf - m. - Philippe Billout    Cléo Bouvier    Théo Bouvier    Fr. René Bouvier

Louis DuLac    Marie "La Coquille" St. Jacques - m. - Henri Petitbois    Françoise Billout - m. - Antoine Bouvier    Jacques Bouvier    Charlemagne Bouvier

Alvarine Bisque - m. - Ferdinand Gurney    Bambi Petitbois - m. - Pépé Bouvier    Monique Bouvier    (Twins)    Lalique Bouvier    Fifi Bouvier    Coquette Bouvier - m. - Maurice L'eau

Ingrid Gurney - m. - Clancy Bouvier    Charlene Bouvier    JoJo Bouvier    Chester Bouvier - m. - Alfreda LeDoux    Theodore "Teddy" L'eau    Hi L'eau    Tilda L'eau

Homer Simpson - m. - Marge Bouvier    Patty Bouvier    Selma Bouvier    Dotty Bouvier    Tootsie Bouvier    Rowena Bouvier    Alfreda Bouvier II    Pierre Bouvier - m. - Miranda Potter

Bart Simpson    Lisa Simpson    Maggie Simpson    Axel Bouvier (Father Unknown)    Dolly Bouvier    Lolly Bouvier    Polly Bouvier    Holly Bouvier